CW01589917

True Love

A Shamanic Healing for the Soul

"True Love for yourself will help you to find a True Love. Many souls are calling for True Love, calling to each other..."

Cover art is a composite based on the Chamber Paintings from www.WingMakers.com, used with permission from James, the original artist. Composite designed and created by Mark Hempel.

Editing, book design and graphic design by Marc Williams.

www.MarcWilliams.co.uk

I wish to thank the Spirit of Sun Bear and Wabun Wind for sharing their healing Medicine Wheel to help **Planet Earth and All Her Relations**.

www.SamanthaWilliams.co.uk

First Edition: by Samantha Britt Beaumont in 2008
Second Edition: Copyright © 2009, by Samantha Britt Williams
All Rights Reserved

ISBN: 978-1-4452-0534-2

Dedicated to my True Love

A Pair of Pears

The summer breeze blows through my hair

And from a tree drops a single pear

And there it sits, all alone

And from the tree comes a woeful groan

As it drops another luscious treat

The two pears finally meet

by my daughter Lhasa, age 9

Table of Contents

One

Why I Wrote This Book

Throughout my adult life, when I went near anyone with the slightest psychic ability to see into the future, I was always asked, "Where is your book? Why have you not written it?"

Over the years, it became a bit of a joke. Would I ever write this book? It is as if the Spirit world was encouraging me to share what I know. To help others to create the life they desire by using a Native American Medicine Wheel and their imagination. Then, they can be their own past, present and future life therapist, accelerating their individual soul's healing processes by accessing their inner voice, or the soul's inner intelligence, a connection to Universal Wisdom, to know the answers to all their questions.

The time for going to psychics is over. We need to find our own way to self-activate universal wisdom, by remembering and acknowledging, that we are magical universal human beings. This means honouring and healing the entire journey of our soul's past. Ask your soul's inner intelligence, that is connected to all living things, to help you find your power within.

This power within, this magical love, to create a good life, shows up in your life when you really love yourself. To really love yourself, you have to know who you really are. To know who you really are, you have to acknowledge and heal the entire journey of your soul. Go back to your soul. Go back to True Love for yourself.

This True Love for yourself will help you to find a True Love. Many souls are calling for True Love, calling to each other, as these relationships can create a special magical love. Magic and True Love are urgently required to help create a good future and heal humanity and Planet Earth.

I have been a Spirit Communicator and Shamanic Healer for over 25 years, and now wish to share my way of healing for your soul. I intend to show how to activate the magic that has been buried deep within all of us to access and heal all our past and future lives, to steer this Planet Earth and All Her Relations, which means every living thing, including the human race, into the best possible future.

I have learned from my own soul's inner intelligence, which I understand to mean that all of my past lives, including this one, have something in common. The same soul has journeyed throughout time repeatedly. This statement may not resonate with you if you do not believe you have lived before. However, this hurdle, once surmounted, expands your mind instantly.

One of the most spiritually enlightening facts to discover is that you have lived here before, at least once. I have never met a completely novice soul, and I am sure there are a few, but the majority of the human race has been here many times before.

The Hindu astrologers believe all of us have had at least 1,000 lives. Wow! If we have stored all these separate life experiences within our being, are you not a little curious to find out what you've experienced in those past lives?

You may have had 1,000 fathers, mothers, sisters, children, friends and lovers. Is all that life experience and knowledge lost, forever? Can you get it back? I asked myself the same questions. "Can all of my past life experiences, memories, lost knowledge and skills be returned to me? Is it possible to be all my past lives at the same time? Is there a way to access this self-knowledge, to become a magical universal human being?"

I discovered that my past lives included living as a:

Farmer	*Witch-doctor*	*Teacher*
Baker	*Tai-chi master*	*Pirate*
Sailor	*Horse whisperer*	*Slave master*
Barmaid	*Fisherman*	*Herbalist*
American Indian	*Shiatsu doctor*	*Caveman*
Monk	*Blacksmith*	*Exotic belly dancer*
Healer	*Hunter*	*Highwayman*
Midwife	*Writer*	*Knight of Templar*
Nun	*Samurai warrior*	*Soldier*
Priest	*Landowner*	*Pilot*

Imagine being able to meet and greet all your former selves from your past lives. What wisdom and knowledge would you be able to rediscover? What skills would instantly be re-remembered and available to use again? Your ancient wisdom is waiting. Are you interested in discovering who you have been in your past lives?

I have personally investigated about 50 of my past lives in the last 20 years. Significant healing occurred, whether I used hypnotherapy or my own imagination in a sacred Native American Medicine Wheel. I currently use only my imagination to view the life, without actually feeling it. I will explain.

Usually, a past life therapist is trained in advanced clinical hypnotherapy. The therapist begins by inducing you into a deep relaxed state, so you can access your subconscious memory and feel the actual experience of being in another body, in another time. You actually step into the body of your former self *(who you were in the past life)* and feel the complete experience on both physical and emotional levels. As it can be deeply traumatic, most people tend to do one life and stop at that. This just bogs you down into one other life. It is a slow recovery process as each life can take six weeks to integrate into your conscious mind.

I have been able to experience this technique to access twenty past lives. Personally, I am fine with this technique, I love going to other times and investigating. Where do I live? What do I do for a living? How do I feel about life, and what my lovers and friends are like? Even small things like what the local currency looks like, or what kind of food people are eating. In essence, it is a live history lesson, experienced in the present moment.

It is very fascinating, even though I was once being eaten alive by rats in the Great Fire of London! I left that life very quickly! Or others, where I was constantly being left by fellow companions on different battlefields across Europe to die horrible, slow and painful deaths.

The funniest life I accessed was when I entered the body of a former self that was in the early stages of being beaten to death by a group of enraged villagers! I was laughing and yelling at them to stop hitting me! They did actually stop to listen for 5 minutes. I explained I was a future self, and tried to take the opportunity to apologize for whatever I had done to warrant such abuse. However, I was strongly advised by the group of villagers to leave, as they were waiting to carry on beating me to death! You see, you cannot avoid or fully change your history, but you can heal it. Can you understand why I thought there must be a better way of dealing with past life therapy?

Over the years, I have been able to teach others to imagine a beautiful Native American Medicine Wheel, creating a sacred place to help retrieve personal information about their past, present and future lives. It works best to imagine inviting, into your sacred Medicine Wheel, the spirit form of every man, woman or child you were in your past lives. It is a very gentle process, they have a soul connection to you.

It allows a certain level of detachment, as we are dealing with your former self. We can also accompany this former self if necessary, and travel backwards in time to view the past life, not experience it. This method provides the same information in a quicker process with more objectivity, helping tremendously, as you will find out, if you wish to use my technique. By taking personal responsibility and healing your past lives *(former selves)*, you can make a powerful and positive impact in your present life.

It is not a question of needing to access lots of individual past lives. It is more about opening up your mind. A couple of past life sessions are encouraged to help easily reconnect you to your soul's inner intelligence.

I have created mass past life healing, where all your former selves are invited at the same time for healing. Once processed, you will be able to access universal wisdom, to answer your own questions and become a magical universal human being again.

This is how you find out who you really are, by finding out who you have really been, and to acknowledge your entire journey through many different past lives, discovering your true self. It is an incredibly powerful Shamanic self-healing tool. But what is shamanism[1]?

Shamanism is an ancient way of awareness, an awareness of the life force energy, an awareness of your soul or your consciousness. It is a term used to describe the practices of indigenous people from all over the world. They were, and are, the healers within the community, known as the Shamans, the Witch Doctors, the Spiritual Elders, also known generally as the Medicine People.

These medicine people are in tune with Planet Earth and

1 Shamanism is a range of traditional beliefs and practices concerned with communication with the Spirit world. A practitioner of shamanism is known as a shaman. There are many variations of shamanism throughout the world. Shamanism is based on the premise that the visible world is pervaded by invisible forces or spirits which affect the lives of the living. Shamanism requires individualized knowledge and special abilities. Shamans operate outside established religions, and traditionally, they operate alone.

All Her Relations. They know how to touch the soul in everything in order to keep a healthy balance within each individual, within the community and therefore, within their world.

For these medicine people, there is no separation between daily life and Spirit, as they know that all things are connected, and that dis-connection equals dis-ease. Although our modern life styles seem very far removed from the experience of indigenous peoples, the needs and expressions of the human soul are still the same in their desire to connect with love and creativity for each other, their community and their world.

For the Shaman, everything is alive and carries information.

In order to communicate with the spirit, soul or consciousness of these former selves, you will shift your own state of awareness by creating a personal sacred space in a Native American Medicine Wheel, in your imagination, in your home, or somewhere in nature to allow Great Spirit and the Power Animal spirit guides to help heal you. This Shamanic practice is characterized by the soul's flight. You make a gentle shift of consciousness, which allows the free part of your soul to leave the body. You can then go backwards *(former self)* or forwards *(future self)* in time via the Medicine Wheel, to retrieve information for powerful self-healing and personal growth.

First, you will heal your past lives *(former selves)*, and if necessary, you will retrieve lost parts of your soul, your healing power or things that you have lost along the entire journey of your soul. Then, as you travel forward in time, you will observe and help your future self to create the life you desire, creating a life worth living.

I used past life therapy for many years on myself to help with a problem. For example at 21, I wanted to know why I could not make a good income. I asked to access the life that has blocked my ability to earn money at this time. Half an hour later, I was sitting in my living room laughing, realizing that I was a very mean and wealthy landowner, who never paid his workers. Because I had commited negativ actions in a past life with regard to money, money was withheld from me in this life.

Over the years, I realized that every single past life I accessed was really awful. My past lives involved great hardship, war, starvation, illness, emotional trauma, and heartache. Severe volcanic eruptions, even floods and major earthquakes also featured regularly. I noticed that I was usually dead and buried by the age of 25.

However, accessing and healing a past life always seemed to solve the present problem. But constantly discovering that I had terrible times in my past lives made me wonder, if I was destined yet again to have a terrible life, or could I change it. Can we really make a difference?

Two

Why Are My Past Lives So Awful?

I decided to go back in time and directly access the last happy life I had experienced.

Oh my God, do you know how far back in time I needed to travel to find a 'happy life'? Would you believe about 14,000 years? I was running around in a colourful belly-dancing outfit back then, and was living in an enclosed city compound, somewhere in the Middle East. We were, as a people, very well educated and peaceful. However, lets just say, I noticed that I had a very low IQ. It was a little disturbing, actually. I thought this is the last happy life I have had on Planet Earth. Something is up with that!

Luckily, I found it very funny. A sense of humour is necessary when dealing with past lives. Make sure, if you are too serious about yourself, to access the past life where you lost your sense of humour. Your sense of humour is actually the ability to love yourself. This ability to love yourself is essential for healing your soul.

I firmly believe that we can learn to love ourselves and everybody else who is here on Planet Earth at this time. How do we love the wicked tyrants and murderers? I have contemplated this. When you have accessed fifty individual past lives, you realize that you, too, have been a wicked tyrant and a murderer in another time. If you do not go around being a wicked tyrant and murderer now, it is because you have learnt on a soul level that what you do to others will, and does, come back to you.

We can find compassion for these souls, and not send out anger and hatred towards them. Imagine you killed someone in a fit of anger. It was an accident. It was not your intention. The local TV news station does a story, and millions watch and judge your accident as a blatant act of evil. Imagine how much misguided anger and hatred is projected out from the public towards your soul, who for your own reasons choose to experience taking a life. If you had killed someone five thousand years ago, maybe only a few hundred people would have heard about it and judged you *(sent anger towards you)*.

I have compassion for all human beings. It is because I know what I have done in my past lives. Would I kill another today? No, under no circumstances would I hurt another! I can assure you that this soul has gained experience by learning about it's past lives. Everybody makes mistakes and all mistakes can and need to be forgiven. If you stop judging others, you will find love and compassion for all people. Then love and compassion will find you.

Did you know that everything that you think, say and feel adds energy to this world? What are you thinking, saying and feeling? What are you personally adding to the world at this time? What are you currently creating? Oddly enough, loving yourself doesn't mean what you might think. You can tell yourself that you are really good at singing, making a living, or that you have a nice car. But this is just scratching the surface and doesn't last long. It is a waste of your time, to be honest. Looking within is where the answers are waiting to be found.

To really love yourself again, means to forgive yourself. Why do you have to forgive yourself? Because, just by being on Planet Earth at this time means that you are experiencing pain and suffering, and on some level, you are a victim. This is a place of victim mentaility, so you have to have victim stamped all over your being to be born into this reality in the first place. Own it, change it, heal it and let it go. This is also the only place in the universe where you can heal your soul, this means you have the ability to change yourself from victim to magical universal human being. How many people actually know this? Just take a good look around. Have you seen any happy vibrant people recently? We are walking around as deeply traumatized human beings.

Only some remote indigenous tribes are full of joy. Their culture from birth works in harmony with Nature. They use prayers, songs and dancing ceremonies to stay in touch with their souls' connection to Planet Earth. By staying in touch with the natural world, they remain natural and their souls receive love. They have the tools to create a loving happy existence.

I was very interested in understanding why all my past lives were so awful. I have been a natural psychic all my life, since a small child. I could see what others could not see. People say there is a veil between spirit and us. I was born without the veil. I was born with my sixth sense fully activated – known as extra sensory perception *(ESP)*[2].

If I stand beside you, or if in my imagination I know your original name at birth and your date of birth, I can automatically receive accurate, personal details. With your permission, I can access your soul's inner intelligence, which, I understand to mean, your true self, your universal wisdom, all memories, past, present and your current potential future path.

If you are lying to me, I automatically access the truth. One woman tried to plead total poverty after I had spent the entire day training her in Tibetan hands-on healing. I said, "But, there is £4007 in your bank account." The woman went white. I was correct. Her current bank statement had automatically appeared in my imagination. I have an ability that every human being can learn. It is part of our future, to be more psychic: hearing your soul's inner intelligence, connecting to universal wisdom and knowing the answer to any question.

As a very young adult of 15, I chose to use my natural psychic abilities primarily for informing people about their future. Then at 24, I became interested in helping others with their health problems. I can naturally see into someone's

2 Extrasensory perception *(ESP)* is the apparent ability to acquire information by paranormal means independent of any known physical senses or deduction from previous experience. The term was coined by Duke University researcher J.B.Rhine to denote psychic abilities such as telepathy, precognition, and clairvoyance. *http://en.wikipedia.org/wiki/Extra-sensory_perception*

body, and look at cancerous tumours, growths or medical complaints of any organ. I can tell people exact measurements of tumours. I am also able to tell people exactly what their doctor is going to say at their next appointment.

In my imagination, I can view future test results, treatments–even what surgery procedures will be performed in the future. I once informed an intensive care doctor of a German drug he should try using on a seriously ill comatose child. I cannot speak German! I had to spell it out for the doctor, literally.

When clients receive their tests results, they tell me that I am exactly right about the size, shape, condition and or medical procedures they have been offered. This really helps people's healing processes. If I know the present and future details together, I help the client to create the best future outcome. So, most can, and do, recover extremely quickly. As long as they take full responsibility for creating this illness, they can un-create it in their imagination. They can travel the path to health that I have seen. As we create our lives with what we are thinking, saying and feeling, staying positive is important to restoring one's health.

I use my imagination to walk forward in time to see the future path and report back what I had seen. I have even worked with the British Police force, helping to discover what happened to two missing young women who were presumed dead. I am able to contact any willing soul, if they wish to communicate with me.

I have been able to astound people over the years. However, people tend to avoid me in the long run. On a personal level, it is hard to remain friends with someone who is able to inform you about what will happen in your future. If someone is talking about starting a new business, and while they are sharing their future plans, I am told by my soul's inner intelligence that it is a complete waste of his or her time, what do I do? Do I tell them?

This is a natural ability. I can decipher the truth, just by listening. Especially, when they have actually asked their soul for the truth, I show up in their lives, give them the psychic information they seek, and most will still remain stuck, repeating the same old emotional drama. Why? Because, unless you learn to reconnect and receive your own advice from your own soul's inner intelligence, the advice of another, however good they are, just does not hold for long.

People are pulled back into their negative self, the high from the information is just that, like a drug, where you need another fix, so you get another psychic reading. There is no inner shift because this is information that comes from outside of you. In order to grow spiritually, you need to get in touch with your own information, by learning to access your soul's inner intelligence. This amazing gift of insight is available if you wish to learn, it is a natural ability of the soul.

I realized that some people are just not interested in acknowledging that everything they think, say and feel forms the basis for their lives. We ARE the creators of our lives, however disastrously we construct them. We must take the credit for everything we experience. Good or bad is just how we label our point of view at the time. You may have a small car crash, which is bad news and then discover that a serious car accident involving many cars happened the next day at the exact time and spot you passed every day. Nevertheless, you are on the bus unharmed, as a result of your car being in the garage for repairs.

You may try to call to my attention to all the abuse you have experienced at the hands of a violent parent, partner, sibling, school bully, work colleague or a string of global disasters created by the fake elite, consisting of all the world governments, multinational corporations, world banking, secret societies and their new world order plans. However, all these things dwell in you, the human being. What you need to realize is we all get to take turns playing the role of the good, the bad and the ugly. Do you know what role you are currently playing? More importantly, how many different roles have you played in this lifetime already?

What are you currently creating? This is important, because we are collectively creating this world that we are now living in. Whatever is happening here is due to the desires of the entire human race.

We are the guardians of this beautiful planet, but we have been asleep on the train. We are too busy judging and blaming everyone else for the problems in this world, and far too busy to actually correct our own behaviour. We must become aware and understand that we are unconsciously releasing lots of past trauma or energy, which is creating future horror for our world.

By acknowledging this blame game, we can learn how to look within and start to heal our entire individual soul's journey. Listen to your soul's inner intelligence, it knows what you have experienced in all your past lives. Your soul knows exactly what needs healing and how to heal it.

Will you miss your destination or should I say Destiny? We need to wake up and steer this beautiful planet to a more respectful relationship with her natural resources. Guess what? WE are a natural resource too.

You may ask why we are creating all these horrors? Human beings have been through many different planetary changes before. We carry this ancient trauma as part of the collective memory of the human soul.

It is the time and the place to discover, acknowledge and release all traumas from your soul. You brought this trauma with you to be healed. Whatever has happened to the human soul can be healed now. Are you destined to reach your full potential? Are you destined to be a loving, powerful co-creator with Planet Earth and All Her Relations?

Not as we are all doing now. We are destroying Her *(Planet Earth)* unwittingly by hating, misjudging and ultimately blaming others by refusing to take personal responsibility for the part we have most definitely played throughout time.

Inside your soul is a library of information on every life you have lived, and what you did in those lives. This includes your dark side, your shadow. You need to acknowledge it. Healing *(loving)* your shadow self will give you great compassion and love for your fellow man, bringing back much needed love to the entire human race (the good, the bad and the ugly).

Acknowledge and honour the entire journey of your soul. Forgive and love your shadow, which can include all of humanity's shadow. We can help our fellow humans in this healing process, together. Only when you love your shadow, can you release the fear to integrate your whole self to become love again.

Why do this? Because if we can go back in time, we can heal our past and shadow self, then we can as a loving and healed individual, go forward into our future creating a better world for ourselves and all of humanity.

The veil will be lifted soon in preparation for *The Age of Aquarius* or *The Age of Humanity*, so all the people of this planet will see what I can see. The natural ability, which all humans have, is to be able to communicate with the soul of every living thing in this entire universe, and to be able to access universal wisdom. These abilities can improve or change your future prospects, by directing your future with a positive and loving consciousness.

Practicing, future self communication allows you to master your life, to acquire the skills and experience to use this technique to push forward into your future, helping to co-create the best possible future for yourself, Planet Earth and All Her Relations.

Now, the best way to view the future, is by imagining calling in your future potential self in say, five years time. See another yourself striding up to the Medicine Wheel. This is called accessing your future potential self. Ask your future yourself, "Where am I living? What am I doing? Where are my personal relationships heading? Am I in the right relationship? Am I speaking my Truth? Am I creating my community? What am I doing with my life?" The magic is that, if you are not happy with the information you are receiving, and seeing in your imagination, you can change it. Because you still have the five years, you still have the time!

You can start with much shorter periods of time, if you wish, then you can begin to set and achieve your short term goals. Be your greatest potential future self now. You will achieve so much more if you stay positive and focused, then you will be ready to create your best possible future. To be part of the magic of life as we travel into *The Age of Aquarius* or *The Age of Humanity*, which I understand to mean living as equals in peaceful harmony with each other and all life on Planet Earth.

I am a true Aquarian. My astrological chart is proof, as I have many planets in Aquarius. We all can learn how to be an Aquarian, or to put it another way learn how to be a Humanitarian. We each need to access our soul's inner intelligence by healing our soul's complete journey. A shift in how you see this world, and how you create your future, is important to remember.

The soul is like God... invisible. Can I or anyone else prove to you that God exists? No. Can I prove to you that you have a soul? No. Can I explain that understanding the point of view of many different life experiences will make you a compassionate, non-judgmental loving, human being? Yes!

We can only genuinely relate to other's pain by experiencing it ourselves, to really know what it is like to kill fellow human beings in a war, to lose a beloved child, to die from a broken heart, or to be murdered, imprisoned, poisoned or eaten by a wild animal. One life cannot give you this depth of life experience and understanding. Obviously. I have experienced so much more in all my past lives, that has not been discussed in this book. That is why I can help others. Whatever your problem, yep, I had that one too!

Look, I am fine. You are fine. Why am I fine? Because I know and accept that I am the creator of my life. I have taken full responsibility for all my creations. This is true awareness, allowing true acceptance and True Love for myself.

We are spiritual beings having a human experience, let us not forget. We need to elevate the human being, to realize that as co-creators of this world, we can be our full potential. To create for ourselves much more than this three dimensional slave mentality, which has been limiting our experience of this world. As Planet Earth's co-creators we can heal this world, physically, mentally, emotionally and spiritually.

We are quite capable of a becoming magical universal human beings co-creating together a multidimensional world instead. We just need to get back in touch with our soul's inner intelligence. To help dramatically change this world. This world will change, whether you participate or not. I have spent my whole life predicting future outcomes. I personally experience in the present, what will be experienced by humanity five years later. Or, put another way, you could conclude that I am currently living energetically in the year 2013 at the time of writing this book. I am feeling extremely happy. This is good news for humanity, the world is a very different place in a few short years time.

However, These changes suggest it is a good idea to practice using your imagination, to stay in communication with the soul of all living things. Seeing a sacred Native American Medicine Wheel in your imagination, or making a physical one in your home, will help you to access your own soul's inner intelligence and universal wisdom that is connected to all souls, whether they're a person, animal, tree, mountain, or even a storm cloud.

Even Planet Earth has a voice, if you are willing to listen. She wishes to speak to the humans at this time. She is asking for our help, our love and our creative energy. I have included a conversation I had in April 2008 with the soul of Planet Earth. She had a lot to say that day. She was in a bit of a bad mood! You may feel like reading this section first in chapter eleven. It allows you to participate and heal Her, simply by reading. It is an example of how to heal, in your imagination, in your Medicine Wheel using Power Animals.

We need to stay alert, and aware of what Planet Earth is planning to keep herself safe. We have all witnessed the massive loss of lives due to large earthquakes and devastating tsunamis, hurricanes and flooding over the last few years, particularly, South-East Asia, USA, China and Sri Lanka.

We need to realize that Planet Earth is in charge of the future. We are like passengers on a train *(future path)* with no brakes heading toward self-destruction. We need to find the emergency cord and pull it now. We all need to get off this train. The more people that get off, by abandoning support of this rat race reality, the better off this world will be.

It seemed that I had a soul contract to experience severe negativity for many years, in this life. This was part of my soul's healing journey and I understand why now.

Three

Fairies, Monsters & Black Magic!

When I was three and a half years old, I lived next to a very old couple who let me play at the end of their garden which was connected to our garden by a small wooden gate.

One day, the old woman told me to go and talk to the fairies at the end of the garden. I obeyed and went to find the fairies. I remember sitting down and asking for a fairy to appear. I saw a very small pale blue fairy appear in front of me. I honestly cannot remember what we talked about, but I was delighted. I ran home quickly, to tell my mum and my older sister, Dee, that I had just seen and spoken to a little blue fairy with very small wings.

However, no one believed me. I was told that there weren't really fairies. This deeply puzzled me, as I had just spoken to one. I remember telling my nursery school teacher the next day, who again told me that fairies are only in fairy stories. I thought, well I can see fairies, even if nobody else can.

I repeatedly tried to see the blue fairy again, but she never turned up. I decided then and there, the next time that I see a fairy that I am not going to tell anyone. As I knew that, the doubt put in my mind had broken the connection. I believed in fairies, because I had seen and spoken to one as a small child. We did reconnect many years later.

My childhood was ordinary, up to the age of ten. I was a regular little English girl, with lots of freckles and long reddish brown hair. When I was ten, my family moved to Zambia, Africa for two years.

I personally, liked living right in the middle of the African bush with my pony, Peggity, that I rode most days. We, as a family, visited many game reserves with Lions, Zebras, Giraffes, Antelopes and many other amazing wild animals. We visited the stunning Victoria Falls, met local witch doctors, and joined in tribal dancing ceremonies. The place was full of strange and wonderful animals, plants and colourfully dressed people with beautiful natural Amethyst and towering blocks of Malachite scattered everywhere. Africa was, and is, amazing.

When we returned from living in the African Bush, my parents bought a very large old house, which they still live in today. From the moment I started living there, I started to see spirits. They would come and walk around my bedroom at night and then they began to sit on me. I could see their old-fashioned clothes, from different times in history. The spirits did not talk to me at first. Now I realize that I was only looking into the past realities of the old house. They were probably just harmless spirits, but I had decided that they were negative spirits who wanted to scare me. Since what we think and feel is what we create, I created a horror story for myself.

Many more negative spirits turned up over the next two years, I called them the monsters. I was repeatedly sat on, touched and paralysed. It was a very frightening and lonely time. It was so frightening that I lived in total fear every night. I could not sleep at all until dawn, and then I would sleep for only 2 hours before school. This happened nearly every single night for two years.

Unbeknownst to me, I was co-creating and experiencing severe negative psychic abuse. When these spirits tried to communicate with me, I was fully aware of the depth of agony these negative beings were feeling. If I had the spiritual guidance and maturity of someone who was aware, I may have been able to stop the nightly terror. However, I was 12 when it started.

My only comfort was a small spirit bird, a white dove. I would clearly see its small flapping wings circling above me. When my spirit bird appeared, I knew I could get some sleep.

I believe the reason I did not go insane with fear was because I did not believe consciously that I was an evil person at all. I was more interested in why these monsters constantly visited me and wanted my soul. They did not give up, on and off for over a seven-year period tormenting me whenever I stayed at the family house in London. I spent most of my time abroad, but as a family, we often returned for the three month summer break, and this was when the negative psychic attacks happened. I was never psychically attacked in any other house I lived in. The worst time was from 12 to 14 years of age, and then again, at 19.

I realized at the age of 12 that something really awful must have been happening, as the attacks would start again when I managed to get to sleep. Other nights, I would awaken feeling as if I was flying around my bedroom. They would drag my astral body out of my body to scare me. It worked. I was completely terrified.

So at age 13, I moved into another bedroom downstairs, with my younger sister, Fay, who was 8. I was regularly paralysed and verbally attacked, when I was totally wide-awake. This was truly horrible. I was terrified of the monsters that seemed to really enjoy scaring me.

Other times, the whole bed would shake. I would be wide-awake and get into the same bed as my little sister. She would remain asleep and completely still. Yet I would be holding onto her, with me, violently moving around. I did not tell my parents, they just thought I had nightmares. In a way I wished it had been that simple. My life had turned into a complete horror story.

Many of our girl friends would sleep over, but never staying more than once. Once, a girl actually left screaming, saying that the beds shake. I found this a great comfort actually, as I thought, "I know, they hassle me all the time." I was validated in my experiences. So yes, I was experiencing strange things, but so were other people, this kept me sane.

During this time, from age 12 to 14, I worked as a groom and a riding instructor. Every weekend, I rode and looked after a herd of horses, which kept me grounded. Being able to work with horses was my lifeline. I completely loved riding them.

During all this time, you would think that I would come up with a protection force of some kind. Praying never work, I tried it. I was still psychically abused. I learned to keep it quiet and to cope alone. My one thought was that I am not evil, so they cannot use me for evil. Interesting perspective!

This was my defence. I remember that I did not cry at all about this spiritual torture. I did not run to anybody. I knew my parents would not understand. I always remembered that no one believed me when I saw a beautiful blue fairy, so I was not going to tell anyone about the group of evil monsters living in my house. Would you?

My father moved the whole family to Penang, Malaysia when I turned 14. I lived a blissful attack-free year in Penang, which is a very small beautiful island in South East Asia, known as the Pearl of the Orient – a stunning place. My older sister, Dee and I, had to attend an international boarding school. The only one on the island was a born-again Christian missionary school. Curiously, I had just spent two years in total spiritual agony, and now we were being ordered to pray before every single class! You can imagine my thoughts on this. God had not protected me at all through those nights of terror. I certainly was not interested in talking to Him!

I drove the very strict Missionaries completely nuts with questions about God, Jesus and the Bible. They could not answer to my satisfaction. I was told to stop asking questions, as I was starting to upset the other students. Oh really? I knew then that they did not have a clue about much at all.

My father's job next took us to Manila, in the Philippines, just after my 15th birthday. No returning to the house of horror in London. Yippee! When we arrived in Manila, we stayed at a hotel that was holding an International Arts Film Festival for famous film stars, producers and directors from all over the world.

I was swimming in the hotel pool, when I was approached by David Hamilton, a well known photographer. He asked to photograph me. I agreed. David was very pleased with the photographs and he actually offered me a two-year modelling contract in France. I remember my parents telling me that if I really wanted to do this, they would arrange it for me.

I am only 5 foot 4 inches tall, a red head, being offered a modelling contract. How bizarre is that? I remember, genuinely considering this offer. Did I want to be a model? I just could not do it. I am a thinker, not an object to admire. I tell you this because, if I had signed on the dotted line, I would have stayed for only a week in Manila. However, I stayed for over 3 years with some devastating consequences for my friends and myself.

It was at this time, aged 15, that I had started to learn how to read playing cards. I did not like Tarot cards as the images scared me. I became very accurate at reading peoples' fortunes. It was very common for the students in my school to come to my house and ask me anything about their future. They had questions like: "Will my parents let me go to the beach with my boyfriend this weekend?" "Will

I graduate?" "Should I go to college in New York?" Typical girls' card readings. I also studied Chinese astrology and palmistry. I even read the fortunes of some of the international school teachers. Funny, a 16 year old giving marriage advice to her English literature teacher!

In my final year at school, tragedy struck again and again. Three of my male friends died in car accidents. Every man I tried to start a romantic relationship with died that year. What do you do with that kind of emotional trauma at 17 years old?

My first boyfriend, whom I had started dating at the end of year prom, died in a car crash on the way home from the beach – he was travelling to have a date with me. The whole school was devastated, as he was a wonderfully happy soul. We all lined up at the funeral to pass by the coffin. I was in a very long line, and very upset. As I approached the coffin, I suddenly realized it had a glass top. Before I knew it, I was looking straight at his beautiful, yet damaged, dead face! I cried a lot that day.

How does one also cope with going to two more funerals in the next few months? I had warned the next one and his passengers of impending death, hours before, as I had a loud voice in my head *(my soul's inner intelligence)* told me that the student I liked was in mortal danger.

I went straight to Manangs, the local bar, to warn Richard (not his real name) and the student I liked. We had only had a few dates. He probably decided that night that I was a complete lunatic, because I would not let Richard get into the car. He was my best friend's boyfriend. I told him that if he got in, he would be seriously injured and the student I liked would die.

In the end, he gave me a very strange look, so I decided to let go of his arm. With hindsight, I really should have just continued to hold onto him! We were, after all, very good friends. Richard broke his back and had to wear a full back brace for nearly a year. The student I liked sustained serious head injuries and went into a coma, dying ten days later. I was devastated, yet again.

The third male friend actually persuaded me to give him back his car keys to drive home! I had seen him looking drunk and he was getting ready to leave the party. I had a very bad feeling. My inner voice, my soul's inner intelligence, was yelling at me, telling me he must not drive home. The last words he ever spoke were, "I promise, I will make it home, Samantha. Please stop worrying about me."

Yes, he had a car accident that night, and died a few days later, when they turned off the life support system. I was so sad and very annoyed with myself. I had given him back his keys! I decided, then and there, that I would always listen to my soul's inner intelligence come what may.

Years later, this very same man's spirit form appeared to me when I was 27. He insisted that I was three months ectopic pregnant. He was very persistent. I listened to him and insisted on an exploratory operation. He was correct. I had severe internal bleeding. His spirit actually saved my life.

Now back in early 1985, aged 18, I graduated early with honours. I returned to England to attend the London College of Printing, a specialist College, as I was accepted to train in Public Relations and Journalism. Welcome back to the House of Horror! I was living with my older sister Dee and her Danish female friend from the Philippines. My parents continued to live abroad, for ten additional years. Dee, started to date a very strange Brazilian man who practiced the dark arts of Black Magic, and I picked up on his sinister energy the minute I met him.

Well, he moved into the house, I had to get him out. But before this happened, he decided to curse my sister, plus, he left black magic spells all around our house! One spell was a picture of my sister's face. He had used a match to burn a weird shape in the paper. Dee had a sore appear that was exactly the same size and shape. We did not find the spell until after the sore appeared, so no autosuggestion could have possibly occurred. He had put the spell under her bed, so that every time she slept there, the sore became worse. This went on for three weeks until we found the drawing.

My parents returned from Munich, Germany to help Dee. The sore would not heal. My mother took her to a doctor on Harley Street. I could not cope with Dee's distress any longer. She was terrified, and I was becoming very concerned. I wanted to help her. I told Dee to stand in front of me. I placed my hands on her face, and I ordered the spells to be given to me immediately. I thought I could deal with it.

Oh my God! This evil entity walked straight into my aura, and I could hear it laughing. It had a coat and hat on. I remember thinking, "Why is it wearing a coat and hat?

What an idiot!" Well, I thought that it is from Brazil, so it is probably freezing, being winter time in London.

I thought because it was an idiot, this would lessen my fear. I really thought I could cope with the silly Brazilian's evil being. I had moved him out of the house physically, and I now needed to get him out of my aura, spiritually. The attacks came in full force every night for many weeks. If I did manage to fall asleep, I would wake up with negative beings around me, trying to pull my soul out through the soles of my feet! What puzzled me was why I could see them standing at the end of my bed in small groups, taking my soul again, like when I was 12. Whenever I was being psychically attacked, my soul's inner intelligence would explain exactly what was going on, to help release some of the fear, but I didn't know how to protect myself or stop it happening.

At the time, I was working full-time at night, running an up-market hotel, and attending college full time in the day. I was completely exhausted. My sister was fine. The sore vanished within a week, and she moved out of the house, refusing to talk about it. I, however, was left with the evil being with a silly coat and hat on. It tried to talk to me, but I refused to respond. I could see and hear it 24/7. My approach was to ignore it, not listen to its constant evil muttering about most people I walked past.

Only my family knew about the spells. Would you go around telling people, at a respectable London college? "Hi, what have you been up to recently?", "Me? I have been looking after my sister's evil entity. Yes, an ex-boyfriend cursed her. I know it is terrible. However, it is okay, because I have saved the day. And, he's still in my aura, so you had better move over a bit, because you're squashing him!", I mean, really, what was I doing? What was I creating!

Luckily, I had a spiritual friend, called Austin, who sometimes drove me to college. He took one look at me and said, "Samantha, you have an evil entity in your aura". I just burst out crying. I was so glad he could see it too. His mother, who was the head of a gospel church, was contacted and offered to do an exorcism on me immediately.

My mother was in London and had to attend. After the session, Austin's mother spoke to me privately, and told me to stop worrying. She laughed at me, and told me I was very clever. Her spirit guides told her that the Brazilian man had offered me a drink at a party, which Dee and I had arranged. She was correct. I had put the drink to my lips, but in my head, my soul's inner intelligence had yelled "Stop, don't drink that!" So, I did not. I poured the drink away. I always listen to the voice in my head.

Because I had not drunk it, he had not been able to curse me. I thought, "How lucky am I?" Imagine being cursed and then asking for Dee's curse as well!

Austin's mother then informed me that I was going to spend my life as a faith healer, healing and helping others. I thought, "Really?" Austin's mother was very religious, and, while I was not, I accepted her gift of a small bible and recited two protection psalms as directed. It helped me greatly. I could not see, feel or hear the evil being anymore, or his monster friends. I truly believed that I was free of this spell.

However, a few weeks later, on Valentines Day, I received a handmade card with strange symbols and calligraphy on it. It looked beautiful, until I opened it and started to read the first line. It said something along the lines of 'your soul is condemned to hell.' I quickly shut the card. I was deeply shocked, because he knew that the spell had been lifted, and he was trying to curse me, again. He knew he was fighting me spiritually too, because the card was addressed to me and not my sister, Dee. I showed my parents, and I decided to just burn the card. I knew if I read it, I would be cursed directly this time.

I decided that I had enough of these threats from, in my opinion, a completely evil person and evil spirits. I also knew that the only way to win this fight was to know, deep down inside, that I wasn't evil, and I wasn't going to resort to using evil *(curse them back)* to get rid of them. I was going to ignore them, give them no energy, and basically get on with my life.

A few days, or weeks, later, I honestly cannot remember, I was standing on the Greenwich Meridian Timeline. I was just waiting for a bus. I felt this almighty thud within my body. It was as if I had just jumped into my body. It could only be described as that.

My soul's inner intelligence then proceeded to tell me a series of extraordinary and very interesting, but quite bizarre, spiritual facts about my amazing life, past and future. I certainly was not ready to deal with all this complicated information, but I was happy to hear what my soul's inner intelligence had to say.

I was told that my mother had actually been pregnant with twins. She did not know this. My paternal grandmother was a twin, so this was possible. I lived, but the twin died very early in the pregnancy. It was a soul agreement. One was born and one went to spirit. Little did I know, during all these psychic attacks, that I always had a twin in spirit standing right beside me. This explained why I was so psychic – I lived in two worlds, at the same time. However, my twin could not help me. My twin just stood there crying. No wonder I never cried. My twin did it all for me, and saw it all. It must have been terrible. By the age of 19, my twin was livid!

The psychic attacks that occurred from age 12 to 14, and the black magic spells at 19, had resulted in what seemed to be irreversible soul loss. My soul passed to spirit, however, I had a twin soul, that stepped into my body and kept it alive, while I passed to spirit, was healed and sent back, hence the feeling of jumping back into my body at the bus stop. When I jumped back in, my twin stepped aside. This is a very rare spiritual event.

I was also told that I had a destiny. I was being given my Original Divine Soul later in this life. I would also be granted True Love. I would have a relationship with another Original Divine Soul in this lifetime. These partnerships are extremely powerful and help create new ways of being. They lead to new levels of existence, to help heal the collective Human soul. I would help others heal their souls and find True Love.

I heard and acknowledged all of this, however, I was really tired of this spiritual stuff, as it was all way too much. Original Divine Soul! Indeed! What was that? No, I needed peace. I had seen, heard and experienced too many things in my short years on this planet. I just stored that information with all the rest. I was very good at controlling what I thought. I had to let it all go, right then. It was not my path to go around telling people my strange spiritual experiences. I never told another living soul. I left home to stop thinking about all these spiritual things. I needed to forget. I knew I needed time to heal. I was 19, and I wanted like a normal life, please?

However, something extraordinary happened. When I was 23, and my son and I were homeless, I was given a house on the Greenwich Meridian Timeline. I thought, "How odd is that?" I had leapt back into my body about 500 yards away, I could have been moved anywhere! It made me remember what my soul had told me.

four

Becoming a Healer

When I was 24 I started to train in complimentary therapies upon recommendation by a surgeon. I had already helped my son Joseph, born two years earlier with a severe foot problem, from having to face years of operations. I wanted to help him through natural means, I studied anatomy and physiology and would treat him every four hours day after day. Due to my spiritual abilities I also decided to approach The London School of Psychic Studies to train in Basic Spiritual Healing. I wanted to go to a reputable college. While I was waiting to be interviewed, I was sitting in the waiting lounge with many other hopeful candidates.

Suddenly, a woman in her forties entered the room, she took one look at me, and went into a complete trance. She pointed at me and shouted rather loudly in front of everybody, "You will go and live as a tribe again, I see you in American Indian clothing. I see you with many horses. You are very spiritual. You are very blessed. You will survive. You have a destiny."

Then she collapsed on the floor! Everyone was rushing

around her. The college administrator was very embarrassed and kept apologizing to me. However, I was too busy thinking about what the woman had just shouted at me. I did not quite know how to take it. I had never seen a trance medium before. Was she a teacher or fellow candidate for the healing class? Or just someone who was wandering around behaving like a complete lunatic? I thought, "What are you talking about American Indian clothing and living as a tribe again? Why am I very spiritual and blessed? I will survive... survive what?" And there was that word 'destiny' again!

Horses, yes, I could relate. However, I had not actually ridden a horse in about 10 years. The rest was news to me. I thought, "I have been away from spiritual energy for 5 years, and I cannot even go to an interview without something totally bizarre happening." I just wanted to be a healer.

A few weeks later, I received a letter from the college. I was offered a place on a different course, that I had not even applied for, starting later in the year. Oh! Had everyone sitting in the waiting room that day, completely freaked out? I mean, she really shouted loudly. We all probably jumped out of our skins at the same time. She definitely made me jump. It did make me wonder. Had I unintentionally upset everyone, as it was only an introduction to Basic Healing? Alternatively, maybe, the woman who went into the trance didn't want to, or couldn't train, with me in the same room?

Were there 10 new students, wandering around muttering to each other, saying, "Why is she going to live like an American Indian? Is she moving to the USA? What is it that she is going to survive? Why is she so spiritual? Why has she got a destiny?"

I actually thought it was all very funny, I mean, I was just sitting there minding my own business. I promise! I did ask my soul's inner intelligence what that was all about. I was told it was not something I needed to concern myself with until I was much older. I was told this planet was going to go through many physical changes, and I was destined to survive all of them. Therefore, I did not need to concern myself. I certainly was not going to move to the USA. Every time I tried to buy a ticket to New York, my soul's inner intelligence would yell, "Don't go there!" So, I didn't.

Months later, the course I was attending at the London College of Healing was very enlightening for me. I was able to use my imagination as a healing and information gathering tool for others. I was able to access fellow students' past lives, as well as my own. The teacher would check the information. I had a gift for past life therapy. I could still access future information as well, and started to read people's futures again. I also trained as a spirit medium.

If you had gone through so much terror as a child, would you dedicate your life to working with spiritual beings, energy and healing? I never really had a choice. The spirits that first visited me were probably kind loving souls. However, I chose to believe they were negative at the time, so I had actually created a situation where negative beings or monsters could turn up and attack me.

Once I had completed my Spiritual Healing and mediumship training, I would have the occasional client who was experiencing negative psychic abuse. If they needed my help, I gave it. I was on a bit of a mission. I was no longer scared of any spiritual being, especially if connected to another person. I had much bravery and love for others. I found out I could use my imagination to visualize my client's house, and stand there laughing at the client's negative beings, without fear. They would immediately leave my clients alone and never come back. I laughed them out of existence! No fear, no energy to stay and cause more mayhem.

Laughter heals everything. Did you know? Laughter and humour break down fear. However, I was soon bored dealing with negative spirit beings. So, I started teaching clients all that I had observed.

Life is really just a question of remaining clear and in your own energy field. This converts any attack/upset into a meeting of minds. I ask spirit questions, I feel no fear, so they do not have any power over me. This is how spirit gets your power. Do not ever be afraid, be interested in them and keep your power.

You have the physical body, which means you have more power. You are in the physical dimension too, which means you are a creator as well – spirit are not. You have the amazing magical creative power. Negative spirit, and negative people for that matter, have only one way of getting power, and that is from you! They are negative. They do not know how to make positive energy, so they steal it from you! So don't share your personal power with them or anyone else. Show people by example, and they will learn to increase their own personal power when they decide to let in love and release fear. It is the same with spirit. Love is always the answer. In your imagination, you can do anything to change your fear to love. Remember, what you think, say and feel creates your future.

So, I decided to change my approach and to learn eastern preventative medicine, Zen Shiatsu and Tibetan energy healing. I wanted to treat my son and other people physically, naturally. When I trained in Zen Shiatsu, I was told by my soul's inner intelligence that whatever is going on for someone can always be treated on a physical level, by going back to the organs. This helped me to approach healing in a new way.

I was bored with dealing with the problems. Let us find a way to not create the problems in the first place! This became my focus. What were people doing to themselves, by creating cancerous tumours and deadly diseases? What was that all about? I wanted to find out. I was very curious.

When it comes to the emotional aspect of the client, I knew that I did not really have time for people that cried and got themselves into an emotional state unnecessarily. This is attention seeking. I was not going to counsel people either. "Oh, it's Tuesday, I have counselling at 1 o'clock. Now, what are all my problems again?" What you feel and speak, you recreate. So do not do counselling. Stop spreading and recreating more future misery for yourself.

Upset emotions are usually just automatic trained responses from childhood. You think this and are automatically thrown into a preconditioned response. You see a spider and run. Why? Because that is what your mother did. Fear is usually passed down through generations, repeatedly. What fears are you recreating that are not yours? Release these fake fears. Find and heal your own fears. Yes, unhappy feelings count and are to be acknowledged and honoured, just not to be used to turn your life into a huge never ending emotional trauma or the 'poor me brigade'.

Whatever has happened to make you sad, just know that if you do not understand why now, in time, you will figure it all out. It may end up the exact reverse somewhere down the line. Stop worrying, everything is always in Divine Order. It cannot be any other way. I know this, do you?

I also began to understand that, if all fears start in the mind as thoughts, then this is the place to stop all fears *(thoughts)*. You have a choice. You can either learn how to control your fears *(thoughts)*, or someone or something else will, like parents, lovers, money worries, an illness, addictions or even a spiritual crisis. The easy answer is to stop worrying, and start creating your future in your imagination. That is where you can actually create the future you deserve. It is paramount that you love yourself and release any fear held in your mind, so you have no irrational fear. This is very important.

However, a little bit of rational fear may be useful, like, "I do not think I should try to leap between two buildings, twenty feet apart, because I will fall and die." You need this type of fear, it's called 'common sense'.

This is why, I believe, we have come here, probably up to 1000 times, and still, this planet, and our world, is a complete and utter mess. We (humans) are a complete and utter mess too! Take a good look around. Don't you agree? We have lost our soul connection to our soul's inner intelligence, which has become silent. We need to hear the voice within and listen to its advice. This is why I believe that past lives hold some of the answers you may be seeking.

When I started to investigate my past lives, from the age of 20, I was wondering why I was always killing people! You see, this whole planet is pre-designed to perpetuate war. We have created and participated in thousands of years of war. Civilization. Oh really? What a joke! We need to start over again, change society, and create one based on compassion and love. This I believe has already been achieved deep down in all our souls. We who are here on Planet Earth at this time have the ability to activate this inner self love and find True Love for our selves and find our True Love partners.

However, we must become healed individuals. Not creating war and conflict via subconscious pain that we still carry. We need healed individuals to co-create a better world. We are fully capable of healing ourselves and Planet Earth.

I discovered that some of my pastlives' action's had deeply traumatised my original divine soul's energy field. I had done some pretty bad deeds. It helped me to understand that my childhood was a reflection of all the horror I had unwittingly committed. When I killed in the name of some silly king, I had a lot of blood on my hands, running around on some crusade in the name of God!

When I was much older, I found all this out through past life therapy. It was in my divine soul contract to discover and heal all my past lives. I agreed to love everybody, which means to love and honour every part of my being. To honour all of my soul's past journey, the good, the bad and the ugly, come what may.

What had I done in my past lives to warrant such spiritual abuse in my childhood? I do actually know! In my imagination, in my Medicine Wheel, I lined up 15 of my worst past lives in a corridor, each with its own door. I opened each door, and peered in to look at the many horrendous scenes of devaluing people as a slave trader, a knight, a soldier, a priest, a chief or a dark arts assistant *(oops!)*. Once when I was a very stupid ignorant farmer, I accidentally re-routed the river, which resulted in a whole village and their live stock dying of thirst. What a complete and utter idiot I had been!

Some doors, I would open slightly, and think, "Oh my God!", And then I slammed them shut quickly in complete hysterics. I actually found it very funny. You see, I truly would never, in a million years, believe I had been so evil. Not ME! However, I had been. Really, what can one do? Guilt serves no man or woman. One can only forgive oneself. It is past, gone, finished. One cannot change the past.

Nevertheless, you can heal yourself and your soul's memory of what you did, so you do not have to continue to punish yourself and this beautiful world, by unconsciously recreating what you hold in your soul, lifetime after lifetime. I, Samantha, would not dream of harming another soul in this life. Not even a mosquito!

All life is sacred. Life is to be revered and honoured. But

I had done some pretty horrendous crimes against others in the past. I believe we have all done this. The present condition of Planet Earth is a reflection of our past life crimes against our fellow humans. The real state of Humanity! Therefore, I can assure you that I have done everything possibly wrong, at least once. Moreover, so have you!

All you have to do is to admit to all of these crimes against others and yourself, from all your past lives to the present self, and heal them. You can heal yourself and find True Love for yourself. Then, if you wish, have a True Love relationship. You will get True Love. That's what you can experience if you face yourself, your past, present and future. I actually know a couple of ways. It depends on how much of a sense of humour you have. You get a choice. Both ways will make you laugh. Both ways heal your soul.

Ask yourself now:

"Do I want True Love?"

I bet you just heard a big "Yes!"

Go on admit it, it's allowed.

It is your soul's inner intelligence speaking.

It is time to find True Love.

It is time for True Love.

If you are creating a life with no love for yourself, do not worry. When you have healed the journey of your entire soul and forgiven yourself, you automatically create this gift. True Love will find you. Why? Because if you have

True Love for yourself, you can attract True Love. Like attracts like.

A True Love may be walking around somewhere. Are you interested in finding him or her? Your True Love is most likely in a very attractive body – someone you will find totally irresistible. He or she is sitting somewhere in the world, maybe even reading this book! I bet you are a little bit interested. I can help you find True Love. I know a way, and it is simple. To find True Love, you first have to create True Love for yourself.

Did you know that every time you come down into a body and commit crimes against another, you are bound to make this right at some point? Therefore, we are all stuck here, repeatedly, never fully clearing our crimes against others. We have to take back our power! The power you seek dwells in your soul.

I believe that most people's souls are preconditioned, automatically, for the holding bay of a Fake Reincarnation, without true awareness. I call this the 'Fake Reincarnation Trap'. We have been consistently tricked into believing that we are free souls, coming and going in Divine Order with the Cosmos. I do not believe that when we die *(pass to spirit)*, that we leave this place to journey into the Divine. I believe as we pass to spirit, that through religion and other types of emotional conditioning, materialism and or spiritual programming, we automatically go the holding bay of Fake Reincarnation, to be reborn here for another miserable life, again and again, stuck going round and round. Getting spiritually nowhere. Weakening our soul with every consecutive life. Feeling less loved and becoming less magical and creative.

Interestingly enough, when communicating with atheist humans in spirit and indigenous tribes, this very small section of humanity never ever visits the holding bay of the Fake Reincarnation Trap. They manage to move on, to evolve spiritually. They continue their Divine spiritual journey across the Cosmos.

Is this why indigenous tribes throughout the last five centuries have been systematically destroyed by the Fake Elite, to ultimately weaken the human soul? Maybe we need to all become either atheist, and reject religion, or go and live as small magical indigenous tribes in harmony with Nature once again.

As an experienced medium, I assure you that most of our relatives are stuck in this trap, hoping to be saved by some so called spiritual leader or some other so called spiritual guru. I have spoken at great length with spirits held there. They do not wish to upset us, so we are not made aware of their terrible spiritual predicament.

They wait, promising themselves that they will be reborn again and have another chance to get out of here, to continue their real spiritual experience, but this world is preconditioned by religion, politics and materialism.

Then add to this, a world of wars and poverty with nearly 7 billion stressed out human beings, making it all too easy, once more, to lose their way. We have all been spiritually losing our way.

Do you really believe that we have lived 1000 lives each, journeyed to the Divine, learned from our mistakes, acquired wisdom and are able to create a better world? If so, then why is this place in such a diabolical mess? Something is definitely not right!

I know a way, using your imagination, to put this right. I know a way to love your present self and free all your past lives that may, or may not, be stuck in the holding bay of Fake Reincarnation. I know how you can heal your soul's journey through time. How you can strengthen your soul, your power within, and discover the magic to create the life you desire.

My way is through loving and communing with the natural world. My way is fun and childlike. My way means loving the spirits of the Native American Power Animals who wish to guide and help us at this time, to help us connect back with our soul's inner intelligence, to access universal wisdom, to help heal the enviroment and learn to love ourselves again.

Power Animals are linked to your soul and want to be your spiritual guides, so you can learn to heal your present self and former selves. It is time to work on healing yourself, as we have lost touch with our spiritual power and our orginial divine souls.

My soul's inner intelligence told me to go back to the Power Animals, go back to the trees, go back to the elements, go back to the natural world. Go back to the Medicine Wheels. The human soul is losing its connection to nature. Let the Power Animals heal the humans. Let the trees heal the humans. Let the elements heal the humans. Let us surrender and be healed by nature, as it is love. We need to connect back to nature, to become natural again.

We need to heal our past lives' crimes against others. I have only accessed 50 of my lives, but I have healed all of my past lives using my imagination in my Native American Medicine Wheel. In my imagination, I am an all-powerful creator. I manifest the life I desire by healing and loving my soul via my Power Animals. This is true power. This is True Love for self.

The reason for using a Medicine Wheel is because you can send love and healing to everything in this universe, while you work on healing your past, present and future lives. It is a win-win situation. It can represent everything in this universe. You can ask the most powerful force True Love, to assist you and heal our beautiful world. The Native American Medicine Wheel and the Power Animals will show you how to create a good future for yourself, Planet Earth and All Her Relations.

First, I want to continue my story and show you how to communicate with your future self, showing how to create a good future for all of us. This is where the real adventure can begin. When we learn to love ourselves and everybody else, we return to our true state of being. ***We are love.***

five

My Soul Exchange

In 2004, at the end of July, I was 37. I wanted to move somewhere in Nature. I was interested in knowing where I would be going. At my home in London, I have a sacred Medicine Wheel made of large rose quartz crystals *(representing Wolf and True Love)* which I sit in.

However, in my imagination, I see my wolf and my lioness sitting with me in a very large and beautiful bright green forest, with large rose bushes of every colour, forming a circle, beside a pale turquoise waterfall. There are many tiny fairies singing and dancing around my violet flamed sacred fire in the centre. There are colourful, magical birds of paradise sitting in the trees. I visualize being there. I am there. This is my sacred universe. Welcome!

I asked for my future self in 5 years time to come to my Medicine Wheel to talk to me. Immediately, I see her arrive. She is striding towards me, smiling. It is summertime in 2009. She is 42, slightly tanned and wearing khaki-coloured shirt and shorts, mountain boots and has much longer hair.

I suddenly felt the huge difference in our energy fields.

This future 'me' was glowing. I remember thinking, wondering, "What is she so happy about?" She gave me the nicest hug that I have ever had. She said that I needed to do a complete soul exchange on myself. Excuse me? What is that?

She told me to stick with the Medicine Wheel and that I would write a book and find my True Love. Oh?

I asked her, "What is this book about?" She replied, *"All the things you have never told a living soul about... Your spiritual secrets!"*

I thought, "What is she talking about?" I did not have a clue, but I promised I would write my book. I would also invent my own past life healing therapy for the soul and help others find their True Love as this was my destiny. She left, really laughing at me. She seemed slightly different to me. I was quite curious. I knew something was going on, yet, I just could not quite put my finger on it. I had even stopped working in healing.

I certainly could not consider myself a trained Past Life Therapist. When I was 26, I approached a highly-recommended college for past life healing. I could already view anyone's past lives, but I wanted to actually take people to experience their past lives. On the first day, the head teacher turned up to give all the new students an attunement to Eagle's Breath. This gives one the ability to take one's clients to different times, in effect, to time travel.

So, five minutes into the class and we were all asked, "Who is happy?" Well, my hand shot right up in the air. I am always happy. Big mistake! The head of college went bananas scolding me! I was happy, to me, life is in the moment, I had answered truthfully. I thought, do not start laughing at her. I just sat in a gold bubble and tried not to giggle. I never figured out why I was scolded.

All the other students took great offence on my behalf. They were complete strangers to me, but lovely. They were all saying they would quit the course. I told them that it was fine. I realized this woman could not teach me and I was not going to complete the course. I got the attunement to Eagle's Breath that afternoon, paid the fee and never went back. A Shamanic friend was able to help me, because she had completed the training course the previous year. I just never received the other certificates.

My soul was my teacher, if I wanted to know something, I asked my soul's inner intelligence. So, by the age of 37, I did not have a clue about what I was suppose to write about. I simply communicated with Planet Earth, very old trees, Power Animals and all of Nature.

No more messages received from someone's long lost great grandmother in spirit. Those days were well and truly over. Thank goodness! Honestly, some people's great grandmothers were so rude! They were always telling me off! I will explain why.

The Victorians were, and are a complete nightmare, because I did not conform to their idea of what women should wear. I liked wearing denim jeans. Sorry! Am I being rude about that ridiculous Victorian black dress you are wearing? No, I would not dream of it. I was like, "Get over yourself! Do you want to help your great granddaughter, or what?"

I use to smoke as well, and this seemed to really annoy them. I just laughed at them. Was I judging them? I now realize that they were all stuck in the holding bay of Fake Reincarnation. You see, before any reading, I would give the client's spirit relatives/ancestors a quick invite to my place. I usually gave them at least three days notice.

Therefore, I always had information ready and waiting. No wonder so many relatives turned up. What I was actually doing was getting them out of the spiritual prison that they had constructed for themselves, via religion, emotional programming or materialism. The holding bay of Fake Reincarnation.

Unbeknownst to me at the time, I was actually offering free weekend mini breaks. How funny is that! No wonder they never wanted to leave my house.

I was very interested in what my future self had told me, but I was not really any wiser about what I should write in my book. I wanted to understand more about this soul therapy, but no more information was made available to me. I was only told I had to wait. Therefore, I waited, and then promptly forgot all about it.

What Have I Done Now?

Out of the blue, in late May of 2005, I started receiving strong images in my head of being removed from my house in a black body bag! My soul's inner intelligence started asking me to do a complete soul exchange healing. What's that? I was also told that it had to be that night!

Please realize, this is simultaneously happening while I make lunch for my 6 year old daughter, Lhasa. I asked in my head why I was being shown my own death. I tried to centre myself and to stop the images flooding in. As you can appreciate, when I get a message and vision that I am going to die, or anyone else for that matter, I take it very seriously. I wanted to stop seeing myself dead in a black body bag. In the end it unnerved me. Therefore I addressed and requested that whoever was putting these images in my head to stop it immediately. It was beginning to concern me. Therefore, I said telepathically, "You are beginning to scare me."

I can honestly say I have not been scared by any spiritual being for many years. I understood all types of energy fields, good and evil - 'evil' is just 'live' spelt backwards, and backwards is how we need to categorize these entities, they are living in the wrong way. They have made challenging choices, and in the long run, they need your love. They are not to be judged by you or anyone. I just treat them all the same now. They are love, however misguided in their present state, they came from love and wish to return to love, they are just a little bit lost at the moment.

Over the years, whenever I viewed a past life for others, or myself, some ruffians would turn up, sometimes looking and smelling horrible. I just gave them love and time and whatever they felt they needed. We would have a chat, then, if necessary travel back in time. Seriously, they loved it. All this happens in my own imagination. Past or future time travelling is, for me, the best way to sort out a current problem for my friends. It is always fascinating.

However, this vision of my body being carried out in a black body bag, like in some American movie, was constantly being projected into my head, and it really freaked me out. Then, I was being told by a very familiar and loving voice *(my inner voice)* that I have to leave tonight. I asked what that meant, 'leave tonight'. The voice said, "See it as a complete soul healing session, and just make sure you release your whole soul."

I was thinking to myself, "Right! I am being told to completely leave my body?" Now, that's a new one!

I am then told that a 12th dimensional being *(what is that?)* will enter my body, as the 12th dimensional being was on assignment to experience the feelings of being human in the year 2005. This could only be achieved by dwelling inside a current human. The 12th dimensional being was on a fact-finding mission.

Oh! I think, well it probably serves me right as I had been asking for the Divine Truth to be revealed to me. I had recently done two past lives which were very unusual and all about Earth Changes *(included in Chapter Seven)*. Something was about to happen, I just didn't know what!

I was starting to see visions that showed my house in London, collapsing all around me. My favourite tree in my local park kept showing me water above my head! This could be explained as an emotional crisis or a physical crisis. It kept telling me to leave London and leave the UK.

This is why I started to communicate with Planet Earth,

I was curious to find out what was going to happen. I had been told long ago that many physical and climatic changes would dramatically change this beautiful planet. I was much older now. Remember, we are the creators of our lives. I was kind of demanding answers from the universe.

I was half laughing when it was mentioned that the 12th dimensional being would be able to keep my physical body alive while I left and passed to spirit. If this Being was going to keep my body alive, I asked, "Can I come back then, or is that it?"I heard a lot of laughter. I was serious, why was there laughter?

I may have thousands of hours of experience communicating with spiritual beings, but I tell you, all spirit beings stand a good 10 feet from me, just outside my sacred Medicine Wheel! I like my own space. Nothing is ever allowed to enter my Medicine Wheel unless invited, let alone enter my body. This was a serious challenge to my normal rules of spiritual engagement.

I was now directly communicating with the 12th dimensional being. It was waiting to enter my body. This was a lot to take in, literally! The being told me that I needed help with the complete soul exchange. I required 12th dimensional energy to create an energy field to allow my present soul to leave, so I can have my next incarnation or put another way my original divine soul.

Unbelievably, I had actually achieved the near impossible. I had worn out and given a lot of my soul energy away, a little at a time, to help heal people. I actually was not aware I had done that. I was told it was all in Divine Order. I had fully realized why I had manifested many problems to make sure I had to stop working as a healer and a teacher.

I had made it my career to stand up in public and talk about invisible energy! The hardest job in the world, and I had found it. I mean, you couldn't even see what I was talking about?

Yes, you could feel it, if I placed my hands near you or on your body, the heat was extremely noticeable. It was complete proof, to anyone who did not believe in healing energy. Some people said it felt like I was ironing them! Nevertheless, it was absolute and total agony for me. I was completely and utterly terrified of speaking in public. I could not stand being in the spotlight. I am an extremely shy person in physical reality.

I had learned how to do amazing healing, using my imagination. To cure all ills. I felt it was my personal responsibility to inform people that we can heal everything. What a big ego!

Somehow, I had also made it my career to spend many years lecturing to complete strangers from different national associations, like nursing, teaching and the Metropolitan Police, to get healing incorporated into their training schedules. Also, I had approached cancer and AIDS societies, along with many other associations for the terminally ill.

Every time someone rang to ask me to do a free lecture my outer voice said "Yes, of course. When?", But my soul's inner intelligence was shouting "No! No! No!". If it had included "or you will die", I might have listened.

When I was 25, I volunteered to set up the first complementary clinic for Alternative Health in a hospital in the United Kingdom. Within three months, I was recruiting voluntary staff. We were massaging and administering Shiatsu and Tibetan hands-on healing to everybody. I was even given a wing of the hospital to expand the clinic.

The only complaint from the hospital's medical staff, doctors and surgeons was that everyone smelled of lavender *(we used lavender oil)*. I also massaged the Ward Matrons and all the nursing staff, radiologists, administrators, ambulance staff, the canteen staff, and the security guards. This made a very positive and powerful energetic difference to the entire hospital. I had student nurses thanking me for 'making' the matrons less stressed out. The wards were transformed to gentle, enjoyable places to work.

Everyone was attending my clinic, but personally, I wanted to get my hands on the sick children and babies! However, for insurance reasons, I was only allowed if I was invited by the parents. So I used to hang around the children's intensive care unit after my shifts. I did eventually start healing the sick children. The hospital had a great vibe. People were walking around smiling. I had created heaven on Earth. It expanded to more therapists joining acupuncturists and reflexology therapists.

With this experience, starting at age 27, I consulted and lectured for many years with top management at the British Nursing Association of Great Britain. I spoke about including Tibetan hands-on healing techniques in basic nurse training. It was very seriously considered. However, management kept changing, and even though I lectured constantly for three years, it did not get the go ahead.

When I was 33, I trained and taught healing to the top occupational therapist who worked with the police teams that dealt with the worst possible of children crimes. Every single police officer was demanding more healing, as it was really helping them release all the horrible images and cases that they had to deal with. They were starting to feel human again.

One therapist had the police officers living in her office, as I taught her how to construct a powerful healing space, all of them had wanted to sit in her office to absorb the healing energy. They were getting on her nerves. She could not get in and out of her own office. They would line up outside her office before their shifts had even started. However, did the full program get the go ahead? Of course not!

Therefore, at 37, I approached the education authorities, and I trained 26 teachers at one local primary school to see if it would make a difference to the teachers and the student body. It did. However, I did not get the official permission to expand into other primary schools in the local area.

Through-out my long healing career, I could tell you about the HIV clients and the amazing little miracles, like completely reversing the AIDS virus many times. I had the doctors own actual medical proof, but no one wanted to know. I did this, healing the un-healable, many times, without collecting any money. I was collecting medical evidence.

I once helped a young 16 year old female hockey player

heal her entire leg. Everyone was so serious, which makes the situation serious. She was scheduled for a complete amputation. A nurse who knew that I had excellent results with cancer invited me as a last resort. I turned up and found it funny! I asked, "Really? You want to be one legged? But you're so pretty!" I made her laugh away her tumour. She shrunk the tumour within days. She kept her leg. She saw the funny side to what she was creating. Used this way, silliness and laughter heals everything.

This is how I healed the majority of my clients over the years. I would use imaginary blow torches to burn out cancer, or golden axes to cut off a complete breast, if they had breast cancer. I would throw the body part up to Great Spirit, and wait for a new one to come down. Then I would stick, sew or super glue it back on, in complete hysterics, in my imagination. Usually without the client realizing, as they were being all serious. Not a good idea. If you think in a serious way you have serious problems to contend with. Remember what you think, feel and say creates all your life experiences. There is even a disease associated with sickle cell, which makes the skin colour lose its pigmentation. Black skin goes white. I had an African client who had white patches all over his chest. I use to give him hands-on healing. The skin reverted back permanently to the original colour. A bit like painting with numbers, we both found it fascinating. How amazing is that?

Did any doctors find it as amazing as my client and I? Of course not!

No, not one association was ever interested in what healing could be done. I contacted nearly all of them. They uniformly turned a blind eye to what I was doing. Rather strange.

Because I suffered terribly from stage fright, the only way I could manage to deliver my many free lectures to the different associations was to tell myself that it was not about what I was feeling and experiencing. Which was a feeling that I was terrified and just wanted to die. Interesting! I discovered very recently, I had been killed for speaking up against the known ways of doing things in a past life.

I did find it funny though. All my friends knew I hated speaking in public, yet I would find myself yet again, on some huge stage, like Brighton Civic Centre, with 300 faces staring straight at me, including people like David Icke *(a true hero of mine)* actually listening to me!

I realised I can manifest anything in my imagination. If I wanted to be in British Vogue, they would contact me, immediately. I could get into any magazine or newspaper I wanted. I just used my imagination and saw myself being interviewed in different editorials.

The Sunday Times, '*Style Magazine*', wrote an article, and nearly 3000 people actually took the time to ring me up. Now that was exhausting! Alternatively, on live TV, 'This Morning' television show with Richard Madely and Judy Finigan, with millions of people watching at one time. It was getting thoroughly ridiculous!

Did it change this world? Not really. I began to realize that this world is not to be healed. This rat race cannot be healed. You cannot heal the system, you have to encourage and inform the people running the system to heal themselves. The system needs to be changed dramatically. I really tried, but nope, it is not supposed to be. I realized that there is no work to be done. Just heal yourself, and listen to your soul's inner intelligence, that's your work.

I really should have listened to my soul's inner intelligence when it came to my career, as it always knew that I was wasting my time. I think that is what my soul had to learn. I now understood that my soul had most definitely worn herself out. I had completed this soul's contract, it was time to go. I had been waiting on some level. I had been preparing myself.

I am then informed, by the 12th dimensional being that I will be able to have my next incarnation after at least three days. My present soul needed time to pass over. I was actually told, "You have to go home to get all of your original divine soul." This is known as a complete soul retrieval.

Okay, so Planet Earth is not my home? How interesting is that! Now that, folks, is proof we humans are alien to this planet, or at least that I am.

I was also told during the soul exchange that I would be given ancient Spiritual knowledge, that would lead to knowing the ultimate secrets of the future of the Human beings.

Well, I was not going to refuse this offer! Would you? It sounded rather exciting! I was also told that in my next incarnation, I would be extremely happy and very lucky. Personally, luck is self-made in my opinion. I had always considered myself a happy and a lucky soul, so I was interested to know just how much happier one could actually get. I was lovingly told to leave my body and that it was for the best. I felt scared, as I knew I would be leaving this world and this reality.

What if anything went wrong? What if this 12th dimensional being changed its mind and left tomorrow? What would happen to me? Would I be left somewhere floating in space?

I am just kidding. I really thought that this sounded just about crazy enough to work! It had Samantha stamped all over it!

Whatever happens to me, I always find it funny at some point in time. This is how one heals oneself. Laughter is a true expression of self-love. We can fill this world with laughter and love. We NEED to fill this world with laughter and love. We need to heal humanity and look after the resources of this beautiful all giving Planet Earth.

I was again informed by the 12th dimensional being, that I have a destiny to experience ultimate love, True Love. While I waited for my True Love, I got really bored, so I went to see if I could heal this world all by myself.

The problem with me, as with most people, is that I needed to learn to really listen to my soul's inner intelligence when it came to myself. However, I was very good at selective hearing, far too busy helping everybody else. It was time to get rid of my very big ego. That was my final lesson. Heal thyself, silly!

I am fully aware that I am the creator of my Universe.

Remember, I had called in my future self, and at age 42, I looked and felt extremely happy. Therefore, I knew this experience would end well for me. I had definitely invited a 12th dimensional being to come and assist me. Nevertheless, I had created this fascinating healing all by myself. I was going to heal myself, yet again. It just included my death and rebirth on an actual physical level. That was all! This time at age 38, it was arranged. Last time it happened spontaneously at age 19.

I got into my bed. I needed to lay down for this! I also knew that unless I believed 100 per cent and actually left my body, it would not happen. The soul exchange began, and a huge ball of energy ran up and down within my body three times. It was so strong, like a jet plane taking off, it actually made me laugh. Then, I was literally catapulted out through my stomach, of all places! Everything became very bright, like strong sunlight. I believe I went right through the sun! My entire being flew through deep space, passing many stars and planets. I was flying towards a huge beautiful blue planet, much like Planet Earth, from afar. Then, I fell asleep.

For the next few days, I could see two versions of reality. I was, somehow, half out there in the universe. I could see stars and planets for days, and it took time to get to my destination, my original home.

I travelled across the universe, and I went to learn about the ultimate goal of each human. It was explained to me that each one of us will, at some stage in our future, be given the opportunity to create our own entire Universe. Wow!

It felt amazing, and it was a deeply beautiful spiritual experience, contemplating what sort of animals and planet life I wanted. I was allowed to choose. To be honest, it also felt very daunting. I asked, "Is it going to be just me, residing over a whole universe? Or can I have some friends?" The answer I got was, *"You can create and have whatever you like."* I thought, "What if I mess it all up?" I was told, *"Shhh... Stop worrying."* I laughed!

It is a Shamanic practice to dwell in two worlds, but this was not for a mere two hour session. No, I stayed like this for nearly seven days. I could feel this 12th dimensional being's energy field. It was rather bossy and reorganized my whole house! It was funny. It threw away most of my possessions. De-cluttering my life, now that was really going too far! It seemed very interested in me. I think I was considered a 'model of a happy human being'.

I felt very peaceful and centred the entire time. Due to my training as a spirit communicator, I started asking questions and got amazing answers.

I was told the following: *"We are all Creator Gods, nearly 7 billion of us, and most of the human race does not know this yet!"*

Just imagine all that enormous wasted creative potential! Running around worrying about paying heating bills! Really! How silly are we?

"I am God, you are God, if that is the word you wish to use. I insult myself and you, if I think that

God is separate from me or better; this is false. The secret to creating is to stop thinking or worrying about all the terrible problems and events that could, or might happen, and start creating, in your imagination, what you wish to experience and see created in this world. The human being is an exquisite multi-dimensional magical being, and needs to learn how to be magical again. The magic is buried deep within the soul. Go back to the soul. Go back to the Magic. Be the magic. Use it to create a peaceful and loving world for humanity. It is time for love. Go back to love."

You see, at this moment in time, many humans are losing their ability to communicate with their own souls, and to find the magic within. The human being has been operating from approximately 10% of its full potential. We can reactivate the other 90%. We can be the magic within. I now understand the 12th dimensional being was my future self. We are all really 12th dimensional beings, stuck in the 3rd dimensional reality limited physically, mentally, emotionally, and spiritually.

We must acknowledge and understand that we can choose to be magical 12th dimensional beings right now. We can choose to create our own universe, right here, right now. This is important. I chose to be a 12th dimensional being, a magical universal human being.

We can start by healing our souls' crimes against others and become love again. We need to create a very powerful energetic and magical group of humans, to help the entire world change swiftly from being limited, to limitlessness. As a healer, I was able to prove repeatedly that anyone can be healed if one wants to be healed. Where there's a will, there's a way, always.

Therefore, it is time for you to decide. What type of future do you want for yourself, your family, your friends, Planet Earth and All Her Relations? Both require lots of love. Create your future now! Heal yourself. Realize it is never too late to start to love yourself again. Are you willing to use your love and creativity to help heal this world?

Do not be asleep, not now. You will miss all the fun! It is time to wake up and to get ready for the party. Who will you be going with? Got anything better to do, than to heal your soul, find your True Love, and help heal this magnificent Planet Earth and All Her Relations?

I bet you don't. Do you?

To get an invitation to the party all you need is to know, to forgive and to love who you have really been, and to know, to forgive and to love who you really are. It is that simple. Really!

So, late in the afternoon, of June 2nd, 2005, I felt a massive thud within my body. It felt like I had just jumped back in my body again. Yep, it felt just like the last time, at age 19. Note to self: I must remember not to give away or wear out this soul this time.

That was more than three years ago. Am I different? Well, my constant desire to fix everyone's problems has vanished.

Phew! I now work in my imagination on myself, Planet Earth and All Her Relations in the Medicine Wheel. I just create Medicine Wheels in as many places as possible all over this world.

Why do I make Medicine Wheels? Since I plan on staying here on this planet for quite some time, it is a powerful way to send magical love and healing to the immediate environment. You can do all this healing on your soul, just in your imagination. You may start to feel marvellous, but when you open your eyes and see you are standing in the middle of a huge toxic rubbish dump, how much fun is that?

Medicine Wheels are an expression of love for Planet Earth and All Her Relations. Together is best – Humanity and the natural world combined.

It has been a strange experience to stop helping people, as I always had. So when people rang up saying so and so has cancer, I thought, "How silly is she?" My ability to hide my sense of humour wasn't there any more. I just could not stop laughing at people and their problems. I had to stop picking up the phone for a while. Who wants some lady laughing at what you have created, when one is terrified of dying of cancer!

I make them a mini Medicine Wheel now, and to date, they are all fine. I just do not get intensively involved anymore. I could not relate to their inner terror anymore. I realized I had none.

I have seen my future for myself. Do you know your future? Do you have one? Do you need to create a better one? Are you happy? What are you creating around you now?

Do you know what you will be creating around you in say, 2 years' time?

Planet Earth needs us to find our one and only True Love – to be in love, to create and to make love. By truly loving ourselves, we are able to love others. With this love we can create a loving world as it is being created by loving people. Simple. You have a duty of finding that special love for yourself. To release this special energy into this world. How else does love become part of life. We humans create all of this world. We are much more tolerant of everything and everyone, when we feel loved.

So, spread your love around. Link your soul with Planet Earth and All Her Relations. Learn to use a Medicine Wheel and communicate with the Power Animals and have fun in your imagination. It will help you to get to know your soul's inner intelligence. It will tell you these beautiful words, *"Hurry up, your True Love is waiting."*

I can show you how to use the Native American Medicine Wheel and the Power Animals to find your True Love. I promise it is really easy, even a child could do it. You can be an unconscious creator and carry on unwittingly supporting systems that ultimatly destroy the human soul or a conscious all-powerful creator who is able to create the life you desire and help others to create by your example and become love again.

You decide. I know what I would rather be. If you need answers to your questions, learn to seek the answers from within because you are love. Love is the only real energy that will create the solutions.

Six

How To Find True Love

"True Love is a pre-destined divine soul agreement that most of humanity seems to have forgotten. We need to remember this soul agreement to find our True Love. It is our divine right and our destiny to heal ourselves, Planet Earth and All Her Relations - which includes all of humanity."

We have all been suffering from spiritual amnesia, we have lost our way and need again to seek our True Love. This is your destiny, there is only one person you made a soul agreement with, to finally experience the life and love you were meant to have. I know a way, it is easy and fun, to help you to find your True Love. It is our divine right to exist in this world with our True Love. Do you want to find your True Love?

Remember that everything you think, say and do creates your world, so you need to start now, by creating the circumstances in your life that will guide you to your True Love. Life is for loving, life was not meant to be hard and full of pain, but we forgot that we are Magical Universal

Human Beings who seek love. This is our destiny, to love, to be loved and to create a loving world. Take a good look around, have you seen any couples who are deeply in love, who respect and honour each other?

It's a sad fact that most couples are not happy for long, the façade wears out, the arguments begin, the children are left to watch T.V. *(their virtual nannies)* and the sadness continues to consume all of this world. The war isn't just in foreign lands full of oil, it's in many households all across this world, where couples decide to blame their partners for their own miserable lives. No one is willing to take on full responsibility for how they are really feeling, they carry on creating and sending out this sadness and frustration.

Most people start and continue relationships for all the wrong reasons. These relationships usually cause more pain than love. It takes a certain amount of courage to face yourself and how you have really been feeling. To admit that you have made a series of countless mistakes, to realise that you have yet to meet and experience your one and only True Love.

The beauty of being truthful is that you are in a place of love for yourself and this is the beginning of truly loving yourself. My advice for people in relationships that are not True Love relationships, is to lovingly and truthfully end these relationships. Tell the other person you are giving them a gift of being able to find their True Love too.

It is important to tell the partner who you want to end the relationship with, because looking for your True Love while in a relationship is not advised as this is dishonest and what you do brings in more of the same, so your life will only get more dishonest.

You need to be in a good place to find your True Love so make sure you are single and free to find your True Love before you start.

Once you are single, you need to understand that in order to create, you must see and feel the end result without being to caught up in the details of how you got there. In this case it would be yourself with your True Love standing beside you and feeling totally in love and happy. This image, and feeling your inner knowing, is what you need to work on. That's it, you need to create knowing that it is already done, by keeping the details open you are not limiting yourself and can create much more easily. The amount of time this takes is a small factor, you need to spend the time doing it, but do not spend time trying to figure out the details of how you will meet, it is not important. True Love is True Love, don't let your preconceived ideas such as "I must meet my True Love through work, he must be tall, dark and handsome, he must have a high powered job", that you learnt in this life, stop you from having and feeling eternal happiness. Your soul knows who your True Love is, you need to access your soul's inner intelligence and ask your soul to communicate with and find your True Love.

You will find that special person and then, finally you can help create a life worth living to help all of humanity at this time. The more people that experience True Love the more truth and love is brought into this world. Planet Earth needs us to find our True Love, as this generates happy, healthy human beings, being in a True Love relationship heals your soul, which heals Planet Earth's soul too.

I find that using your imagination and a Native American Medicine Wheel sets the stage for spending time sending love to yourself and your True Love. It is one way to prepare yourself and your True Love for your relationship. Why not spend 10 minutes a day visualising, or sitting in a real Medicine Wheel and calling to your Wolf to help you. In your imagination, invite your True Love and their Wolf into the medicine wheel, get the Wolves to play together. Doing this meditation daily is a great way to visualise your True Love and to be on the path to finding them. Also, remember that how you are feeling adds to your creation, finding your True Love is not serious or hard work, it is a loving and fun experience. Right? Why create a seriousness and a heaviness to the relationship before it has arrived?

As I have already mentioned, I use my imagination to create what I want to turn up in my life. If I want to be on T.V. I see myself on T.V. I don't worry about "how" I am going to get on T.V. that part I leave to the unfolding beauty of life.

The reason I took so very long to actually find my True Love, was because when I was younger I didn't actually understand that feeling upset that I didn't have him was the best way to keep him away from me as I was creating this reality for myself. Yes, I admit it that when it came to relationships I did the poor me brigade, I searched my past lives for answers, but I never actually asked out right. "Can I have my True Love please? Silly me, I told you I can be a bit slow sometimes. It took me a while to realise it's quite simple really. Just apply my creative techniques and then see, feel and create the end result - a relationship with my True Love.

When I did the Planet Earth reading in April 2008, she explained to me that she wanted the humans to find their true loves as this is what is missing in this world, so I started writing this book, and I started to get my life in order and begin the wonderful, and happily rather short, journey to finding and meeting my True Love.

Here is the story of how I created the right circumstances to call to my True Love. It is a personal story as you will see, but the most important part is to show you what I did, and how I used my imagination to find him, so you can use this way of creating to receive the ultimate gift of True Love. I ask that you go with the flow, if you want True Love then read on.

A True Story

This is a true story about True Love. Even though I was informed by a psychic at the age of 24 that I would have a True Love relationship, it didn't actually happen until I was 41. When I met Marc, we both recognised each other from a meeting that happened one summer in Glastonbury, 13 years earlier. It also, transpired that we could have met 9 years earlier due to our work in Television, it seems that fate was trying to help us. We were destined to be together, we just kept missing each other.

I had helped many friends and clients using past life therapy sessions to find their true loves, now it was my turn. I started to spend a small amount of time every day using a Medicine Wheel in my imagination and visualising and communicating with all my Power Animals, especially Wolf and Coyote. Within a few days, I actually woke up from a deep sleep as I was convinced I was being kissed. Next, I started to feel the presence of a man standing at the end of my bed, smiling at me. I nick named him the invisible man and doctor who, he seemed to turn up most nights. I knew this was his soul/spirit coming to visit me, as I had asked my soul's inner intelligence to connect us. It seemed to happen very fast. I began to imagine cuddling him in bed as well, when I went to sleep at night. I would even start laughing as I knew that we had made the connection on some level at last. The more I used my imagination, the stronger these feelings came to me.

Next, I used my imagination to journey to different parts of the world holding his hand while we flew across valleys and continents on my Golden Eagle *(mental self)*, to help us connect mentally, or rather telepathically.

We would also race our Golden Eagles across the continents, he usually won!

I would ask my Coyote and Wolf to go and connect with his Coyote and Wolf, to help both of us to get ready for each other on a emotional level. I noticed that our Wolves were always together and very happy to know each other. Our coyotes were also friends, but I needed to give violet healing to my Coyote as she was rather shy. His coyote was quite a lot bigger then mine, so I knew he was good with his emotions, meaning that he felt comfortable with his emotional self, I needed to be healed emotionally as I was a thinker and a bit cut off from my emotions at times.

Every day, I always made some time to be with my True Love, whether it was walking through a forest or swimming in a beautiful river, or laying under the stars at night. I literally created a love story in my imagination. I saw us laughing and talking, and sometimes just holding each other, always somewhere beautiful in nature.

Sometimes, I would use my imagination to visualise a rose quartz medicine wheel, and then I would wait for him to turn up. Many times he was already there waiting for me.

I even built a tee pee in the middle of the medicine wheel and furnished it with colourful blankets and soft furnishings, to give him regular Shiatsu massage treatments as well.

I once entered the medicine wheel in my imagination and I found Sun Bear there waiting to marry us. My True Love had made a bridal head dress out of the stars in the night sky for me. I was very touched by his gentleness and romantic nature. I started to realise that this process had two creators, not just from myself, but also from my True Love. We were communicating via a True Love vibration.

It was an extremely romantic and fascinating time for me. I was careful to keep his image neutral, as I didn't know what he looked like or what his name was. I decided to just use my imagination like a meditation session to send love and feelings to him. I knew something was happening because once we had been spiritually married, I started to experience deep feelings of love and happiness that could only be described as True Love, this carried on daily for about three months.

I had just finalised the first version of this book *(This is version two)* and had joined an alternative lifestyle internet forum that was recommended to help promote my book.

I had quite a lot of interest from the forum from people who wanted to buy my book. Marc, was one of these people and was the first person to actually order and read my book. When he read my book, he decided to order a Power Animal Reading from my website. When I was doing his reading I realised he was a very kind and beautiful soul. I posted him the reading and it affected him greatly, he was very happy with the reading and wanted to learn more from me.

Mean time, I was very busy with the book launch and became very dishearten about my True Love, I was wondering where he was. Just as I thought "oh no, I have been spending all this time creating and nothing has happened", he had actually been in my life emailing me for weeks. He told me he wanted a Shiatsu treatment and to learn more about the Medicine Wheel. Because he lived a few hundred miles away we had agreed to meet when I was visiting a friend who lived nearer to him. I was a little curious, yet I hadn't really realised at this point that he was my True Love. I remember, as I walked to met Marc at the train station, that I wasn't nervous at all, I was waiting for the nerves to come as he was an extremely good looking man. I had a hunch he maybe my True Love, but I wasn't going to assume anything, as I am a professional therapist. I had never ended up dating any of my clients in the last 20 plus years, so I wasn't inclined to think that clients were potential boyfriends.

Also, Marc had a long standing health issue that seemed untreatable with conventional methods, this was my focus at the time and this is, I believed, why he contacted me. As I turned the corner and started walking towards him, I felt an ease of energy. We walked up the road towards the hotel that I had arranged for him. I started the Shiatsu treatment and after a few minutes I started to experience a great amount of energy coming from both of us, feelings of great love washed over me, it was getting stronger and stronger. I couldn't concentrate, so, even though I had met him only 20 minutes before hand, I just blurted out "Do you want a relationship with me?"

He was laying with his back on the massage table and was a bit shocked by this question, however he had written a beautiful poem for me and proceeded to tell me that over the past few weeks since he had read my book and received my reading, that he had fallen in love with me. He couldn't explain it, he just knew he loved me and had decided that even if I didn't want a relationship with him, he was going to love me anyway. I stopped the treatment, and we just hugged each other for a long time. There was no uncomfortable feelings, just True Love for each other. It was amazing to think that we had fallen so deeply in love before we had even met, this is True Love. I found Marc very attractive, not only physically, but emotionally, mentally and spiritually, as I knew from his psychic reading what he felt about life and this world. I have spent my whole life, all 41 years of it, hoping to find someone to love, but it never worked out, because I hadn't asked for my True Love. Once I actually asked, it took me a matter of weeks to connect with him, and a few months before I met him. I found my True Love by using my imagination in my Medicine Wheel and asking my Power Animals to help me. You can do this too, you can have True Love.

All you have to do is know that it is your divine right, it is your destiny. It is time to honour your divine soul agreement. Go on, find that special soul who agreed to love you. It's time for True Love.

Seven

Healing My Past Lives

Before I explain and impart my knowledge of Medicine Wheels I wish to share two of my past lives, as they are very unusual. Both have relevance to what I believe we are about to experience, yet again. Both past life experiences were accessed via my Medicine Wheel at the same time, a few months before my soul exchange. As I am practiced at past lives, I can switch and be in the body of the former self.

Earth Changes

In my imagination, I start to walk in nature to my special place in the forest to my Medicine Wheel. In my mind, I asked if I can enter my sacred Medicine Wheel to communicate with my Power Animals and access a past life. I received a strong, "Yes!" in my head.

As I waited, I saw a beautiful elegant man arrive. He was about 7 feet tall and dressed in a flowing cream robe. He had an air of beauty and grace. He asked me to accompany him, and to travel back in time.

In my imagination, I started to fly down a time line,

holding hands with my former self. We magically travelled back thousands and thousands of years. When I felt like stopping, a door appeared, which I opened and we both entered into a different time.

Immediately, we see a set of buildings ahead of us, and we started to walk together down the main passage between the sandy-coloured buildings. It was a warm and pleasant climate. Everywhere we looked, people were talking in small groups. The thing that struck me the most was the air of calmness and happiness. Everyone looked well-dressed in immaculate cream-coloured clothes. Most of the conversations included much laughter and giggling. It was a happy place.

As I walked towards the last building, I noticed a young woman coming to meet us. I knew she was my wife, and we were very happy. When I entered my house, I remembered that we had many identical sons *(cloning?)*.

I was wondering if that place was actually Planet Earth. I think not. Everyone was so happy! Ha ha! I didn't ask at the time.

I asked in my imagination to go forward in time to see when something significant happened. The next thing I know, I am in bed *(as the 7 foot man)* with my wife, and I am having a horrible dream about earthquakes and flooding. I see many people lying around not moving. I wake up and tell my wife, who refuses to understand my concerns.

I discover that this society creates everything by thoughts, including the weather and the crops. They are at their manifestation peak, all are being catered to, and there is no such thing as a problem, sadness, pain or suffering.

Over the following months, I experienced these visions more and more, and my whole being started to change. I even looked different, because every night I lived through the horror of a great danger coming to my family and people. What nightly terror!

My wife could not understand and asked me to stop telling her about the dreams. I went to the other men of the village and they all sent me love, but shook their heads. My reputation started to slide, and after what seemed like a long time, I was considered an oddity and rejected by my society. I started to experience great sadness, as I know that life was going to change but no one would listen. I decided to go into nature; I talked to the trees and they told me something big was going to happen, the birds and all the animals told me that this was so. They were moving to higher ground, all around me, and I knew the animals were leaving. I told the children to bring their families, to come to the caves, if the ground started to move. I headed to the caves to wait for the others.

I waited for days, and then I felt a shimmering in my body. I looked down. I noticed that I had begun to dissolve my physical body, and I became invisible. But, I was still standing in the cave. A massive noise started in the distance. I walked to the cave entrance and I saw small groups of women and children running quickly towards the caves, they ran straight past me *(still invisible)*, and the noise and the earthquakes started to shake the entire planet. For three days and nights the noise continued, but we were all safe in the cave. On the third day I started to become visible right in front of everyone. My sons had made it to the safety of the cave, but my wife was never seen again. I was extremely upset and distressed with myself, because I felt I could have done more to save the men of the village.

I had seen enough and exited this past life. I journeyed back down the time line and re-entered my Medicine Wheel. This poor man's loss was so great. Yet he had saved lives and life did go on, even though it had changed the climate and landscape dramatically.

Next, I heard my inner voice telling me that I had always chosen to reincarnate at times of great change and my mission, should I wish to remember it, is to go and clear my past life in Atlantis too.

Atlantis

Well, in my head I thought, "Atlantis, yuck!"

At that stage of my life, I can honestly say, I had never read anything about Atlantis. If I heard the word, Atlantis, I thought it was a load of rubbish. I did not want to talk about it! That should have been a big clue! I was still in my Medicine Wheel and I decided to follow the advice to access my past life in Atlantis. I waited, and then I noticed this young woman with long reddish brown hair and a really cheeky look on her face. As she got nearer, I noticed she looked exactly as I look in this life. She ran up to the Medicine Wheel and started dancing for joy. What was going on?

I was asked to journey down the time line to the time

of Atlantis and when it felt right, I stopped and walked through the door. I immediately became the person I was, my former self. I was being held by two strange looking men, my hands were tied behind my back and I was a prisoner. I was really struggling with these men because I wanted to really annoy them. I did not feel scared at all, I was elated.

People had listened, was all I could think about. As I was about to be killed, I did not care. The exodus was already happening. The people were fleeing to the mountains and the caves and would survive the coming disaster.

You see, the race of beings that were in control in Atlantis had changed the balance in nature and the repercussions were huge. I had listened telepathically while being invisible at the secret meetings and had learned of their truly evil plans for the human race. I stood right in front of them, and they did not even know. They were so stupid!

The psychics were telling people the truth that the experiments had gone too far. They were dishonouring creation and a massive disastrous flood would cover Atlantis and most of the globe. Planet Earth *(She is the boss, you know)*, has had enough and was going to clean this mess off Her surface in one almighty jump.

I had been caught and sentenced to physical death, and my soul would be put out of action, permanently, for supposedly spreading lies and treachery. But I knew they wouldn't manage to get it right, they were so stupid! I was taken to a room with a very big crystal overhead, which they had commandeered, from the good Atlanteans!

All the crystals were inverted, they had been changed. I was bound to a large table. They used another crystal to slice up my body, much like cutting slices of ham. As it was done with a crystal, most of my soul was somehow captured. It was then stored within a small clay vase, and sealed with an incantation, not the good sort.

I was part of a group dedicated to stopping the bad guys. We nearly all got captured. I was one of the last to be found, as I could make myself completely invisible. I will definitely ask for that invisibilitiy skill back, it may come in very handy. I was so cheeky, I drove the evil power hungry beings completely nuts. I was very happy about that.

It had been previously agreed, in case of being captured, to give a small piece of hair *(this carries some of your soul energy)* to another member of our group who escaped. This guaranteed a safe passage out of this reality, when passing over to spirit. Hence, this was why I wasn't concerned about being killed. I continued to have more future incarnations. However, since most of my soul had been captured, I didn't create many good lives.

So, I saw my former Self die, it was a real mess, but the strange thing was, it felt fantastic. I asked why and was told that she was so happy to help rescue all the people of her tribe. She had remembered another life when she had only saved a handful. This time, the number would exceed 3,000. She was ecstatic, but she would not live to see this future. But she didn't mind, because she knew she was more than her body. Also, most of her friends had been captured. She had helped by organising the humans to go to a safe place, to ensure the real human race survived, and that was all her soul contract required of her in this life. She knew she would come back, some time in the future.

Healing

I returned to the Medicine Wheel and saw this 7 foot man and this girl from Atlantis, who was my exact double, beaming with happiness. I looked first at this man, my former self, and I asked him into my Medicine Wheel to receive healing from me. And as he entered, a huge explosion of colourful light fell around us. I asked what I could do for the man. He asked to be healed of all the pain and suffering which he had experienced as a pioneer and a visionary, as all the visions of destruction still played heavily in his mind. I used healing energy and love and filled him with light and peace. He then vanished into the violet healing mist.

The girl from Atlantis asked for healing of the physical body. She asked me to go and find the clay vase that holds part of her Original Divine Soul, as it was time to go and free her soul. This was very important to her. I agreed.

I called to Great Spirit and was shown a small cave under an icy ocean. I dived in, and swam to what looked like temple gates. I easily glided through the gates, and entered the ancient scrolls room. At the back, in a small side door that leads to a hidden cave, I found 40 vases with seals placed on them. Ancient black magic was used to capture the whole group. It was to hold the souls so they could not go back home to the Divine to pass over information and experiences. Its purpose was to prevent them from warning others about what was really happening to the humans.

I magically asked, in my imagination, if I can save all the trapped souls in the vases, and I am told that I can. It is part of my group soul contract, that whoever gets out first, they can free the rest. I was obviously the first one out. I journeyed back with these precious souls in vases and brought them into the Medicine Wheel. Together, we asked Great Spirit, Great Mystery, Planet Earth and All Her Relations to break the evil seals. A great fire bolt hit the vases and smashed them, releasing all those precious souls.

As this happens, 40 beautiful souls of all colours float up above the Medicine Wheel. They hover for a split second and smile at me, and then these beautiful beings suddenly depart, all at once, and fly off in all directions. This is classed as a mass soul retrieval and 39 people on Planet Earth have had their souls returned to them. I had done it, at last, my Original Divine Soul had been freed and healed.

I was informed this was my Original Divine Soul. Original Divine Soul means a whole soul. Not shattered and scattered, as most souls are at this time. At last, I could heal my entire soul. I sent her back to the Divine into the violet healing mist. I use violet healing mist, because it protects and heals the emotions. I thanked all the Power animals, Planet Earth and All Her Relations. I finished the past life. I now know this past life healing was deeply connected with my soul exchange, which happened soon after.

The girl from Atlantis *(my former self)* was free to go to the Divine, to continue her soul's journey, which was to be my next incarnation. That's why she looked just like me. I am a bit slow, sometimes. At the time, I thought it was just another wacky life. I have seen many, some are not of this world. We are so much more than what we can actually comprehend at this time.

My spiritual and life experiences have taught me that it is best to first work on healing yourself. Trust me. It is all about how you treat yourself. This is what really matters. Are you kind, loving and forgiving? Go and heal the entire journey of your soul. This is a way to heal your soul. It is my healing way. It starts with compassion for yourself and everyone who is here. Because, you co-create this world, by your thoughts, feelings and actions.

We are the creators. Remember it is up to all of us. Connect with your soul's inner intelligence, heal your soul and learn to access *Universal Wisdom.*

Create a life worth living.
Create a planet worth living on.
Create a universe worth living in.

Life is good for me. It can only get better in my imagination, as I know all things are possible. Do you?

Eight

An Ancient Way Of Awareness

What Is A Medicine Wheel?

According to Chief Sun Bear, the sacred Medicine Wheel is an Earth-based ceremony and tool. The Medicine Wheel appears to be simple, a structure of up to 36 stones. Yet there are untold levels of meaning to the simple circle.

The Medicine Wheel of the past served many purposes for the native people of the Americas. They were places to pray, meditate, contemplate, strengthen connections with nature and come to a high degree of understanding of one's self and the relationship with all of creation. Take the first step to love and become your own Shaman.

How To Work On Yourself With Power Animals

When I studied the Medicine Wheels of Sun Bear, I discovered that his philosophy was that all people are allowed to use the Medicine Wheel, whether you are Native American, Irish, French or Chinese. He believed deeply that all tribes of the world can unite and live in peace.

"The Medicine Wheel forms a Circle. A Circle has healing power. In the Circle, we are all equal. When in the Circle, no one is in front of you. No one is behind you. No one is above you. No one is below you. The Sacred Circle is designed to create unity. The Hoop of Life is also a circle. On this hoop there is a place for every species, every race, every tree and every plant. It is this completeness of Life that must be respected in order to bring about health on this planet."

Dave Chief, Oglala Lakota

In the beginning, when the US was just forming, the first thing the invading Europeans did was destroy all 20,000 American Indian Sacred Medicine Wheels, because they held all the **Ancient Sacred Power** of all the tribes of the Americas. They destroyed them all, their magic, their love and their connection to nature.

According to Sun Bear, you make a Medicine Wheel and wait respectfully for your Power Animals. It was all very deep and serious.

When I first did this ceremony, it was the opposite of serious. The Power Animals were turning up in outrageous outfits and they were hilarious to talk to. In my imagination, I was receiving extraordinary comical sights that made me really laugh.

I was actually a bit concerned, as I did not want to be disrespectful towards this great spiritual power. The Golden Eagle is revered by all the different Native American Indian tribes, the same way that Jesus is revered by the different Christian churches around the world. I began to realize that my sense of humour had actually made a deep spiritual connection with the Power Animal Spirit Keepers.

Great Spirit told me that the Power Animals would be happy to turn up for my clients and show them, by reflecting back to them, their 36 personal states of being in a humorous, comical and healing way.

Each Power Animal represents a different part of the soul or aspect of your life. This healing method can be great fun and can have most people in hysterics. The shortest path to self-love is to laugh your way there.

Sometimes, a part of your soul, or Power Animal, may not want to talk to you, and may not even really like you at the present time. If this happens, apologize to the Power Animal, which as already mentioned, really is a certain aspect of your soul. Make an agreement to change. Tell it you will be more loving towards yourself. Give your Power Animal love for the future. Give it a cuddle. It wants to be your friend.

Once, a Golden Eagle *(your mental self)* was carried into my Medicine Wheel by Great Spirit, and it was in a large leather bag, all tied up in a neat bundle. When I untied it, I found a very sorry looking collection of Golden Eagles bones. That was it!

This represented one of my female friend's state of mind. I remember saying to my friend, "Well, you have certainly done a good job of looking after your mind, haven't you?" This person thinks and worries way too much. Look, there's only a few bones left.

We got my female friend to call on healing from Great Spirit to completely bring the Golden Eagle back to full health, and it grew organs, muscles, feathers, a beak, eyeballs, etc. It was very fascinating to watch, and of course, it took lots of love.

I told her to send healing every day to her Golden Eagle for a while. This meant visualizing her Golden Eagle, in her Medicine Wheel, for a few minutes each day. She must feed it, talk to it, stroke its feathers, go fly around the world on its back, if she wished, she had to remain in daily contact. She gave it hands-on healing too, along with healing violet mists, rainbows, and gold glitter. She went for it. She could decide how to heal her Golden Eagle. This is how she learnt to stop worrying. Her Golden Eagle was very grateful. Actually, all the Golden Eagles were very grateful.

Most people's Coyotes *(your emotional self)* are in a confused state. Some pretend they are dead. I tell them that I know they aren't really dead. They just lay around acting dead, I stand there looking at them, going, "Get up and stop being so silly!"

Sometimes, they tell me to go away. It's so funny that I tickle them. I get the human self to send them courage and to go and talk with their Coyote. This is an extremely common condition of the emotional body. Most people do feel dead inside. Let's heal that one. Once, I saw a completely burnt female Coyote laying on the ground, near a volcano. She was all black and crispy. I thought, "Now, you're a complete drama queen!"

Some people's Grizzly Bears *(your spiritual self)* are very sick and act very strange. What weird religious teachings some people learn. If your Grizzly Bear runs away, (most run and hide) get it to come back. Explain that you know that they are not very well, and that you are going to heal them, in an instant. The Grizzly Bear doesn't need to give you permission, because you are actually looking at your own spiritual self.

In your imagination, give pure water, herbs and berries. Spend time hugging all that soft brown fur. Ride through the wilderness on the Grizzly Bear's back and feel the sun on your face, or visit the ancient Bear Spirits cave and ask for healing.

Again, visualise using hands-on healing, imagine pale pink healing mist flowing from your hands into the Grizzly Bear for unconditional love. Shower with different coloured rose petals for love. Give a necklace made of clear quartz and turquoise to protect and strengthen the soul energy. Use your imagination to give love and healing to your soul, through your Power Animals. Watch it get well very quickly. Be your Grizzly Bear's friend. Be your own friend.

White Buffalo *(your physical self)* is born white, but grows up to be brown, tan or black. It also represents your future. If the White Buffalo is an extremely large Power Animal, congratulate yourself, this is a good sign. You have a great and prosperous future. However, it is very common to see much smaller White Buffalo. In the wild they grow to 8 foot tall. The worst case I have encountered, was a White Buffalo the size of a baby mouse! I was like, "Will this man even make it home, today?"

I gave this man, in my imagination, an air pump to blow up the White Buffalo. It made him really laugh. He's fine now. Still alive, with a regular size White Buffalo, he keeps track of it.

Know your weaknesses. Strengthen the Power Animals that appear very small. Pay special attention to the four directions, Golden Eagle *(your mental self)*, Coyote *(your emotional self)*, Grizzly Bear *(your spiritual self)* and White buffalo *(your physical self)* as these four main Spirit Keepers are very powerful and can help you stay grounded and balanced.

Some people are lazy, so, when you call their Deer *(which is your ability to take action)*, you may have quite a challenge. Once, a Deer was hiding behind a tree. She was standing upright, like a human and running between the trees. I was laughing and telling her that I could see her. She was adamant and told me, that I couldn't see her, and I said "But we are having a conversation!" She gave in and came to the Medicine Wheel to be healed by her human self.

When you are looking for Snow Goose *(which is your ability to create the life you desire)*, you may find a very worried and stressed-out bird, with broken wings, covered in dirt and in need of some self confidence. This world, or rat race, is not for the faint hearted. Snow Geese are always crying and are usually weak. Some turn up with dark glasses on and whisper that they are hiding from life. They have given up on their human self. People are very good at giving up. Give it a hug and encourage it to cheer up, promise that changes are coming, and that you want the Snow Goose (or put another way, your soul) to give you time to create a life worth living. Tell them you have new tools, a Medicine Wheel, to call Nature and all the Power Animals to show you how to find True Love for yourself. You now have new abilities available to create all that you desire.

Wake up to your true power. Become a magical universal human being.

Go and find your Coyote *(your emotional self)* and love it constantly everyday. Imagine walking in nature through the trees by your Medicine Wheel. Make friends by cuddling its fluffy fur. Give it hands-on healing. Remember that pale blue *(peace)* and pale pink *(love)* combined make pale violet *(protection)*. Play with your Coyote in your imagination. This will cheer up your emotional self. I mean, it's not as if you have to actually feed it and take it for walks, right?

Also, tickling your Power Animals always seems effective.

Or tell them a joke, meaning you, the human, go and read some jokes, or read a funny book. Go and spend time with a funny person, resolved to cheer yourself up. If you decide life is funny, guess what? Life gets funny.

By making it funny, you start to feel better. This world is full of worry. Worrying creates more worry within this world. Now, laughing adds more laughter to this world. Laughter breaks down worry. Create a better future world for all of us. Life is very simple. Bring it back to basics. What you spend your time experiencing is what you bring into your tomorrows.

Just go play with some Power Animals. Pick the ones you really don't like first. Many people hate Snakes *(your ability to transform yourself)*. Anyone can play with Dolphins *(your ability to be honest, pure and peaceful)* and Turtles *(your ability to heal this planet)*. Go and love your Snake. Find your Snake and make sure it doesn't eat your Mouse *(your ability to organise your life, introspection)*. I am joking! Power Animals do not eat each other, they respect each other. Remember to become childlike again. That's the way to do it. You need to play with this.

I was going to call this book *'The Art of Complete Silliness'*. However, I don't believe people are ready to acknowledge that we all need to be a bit silly. Life here on Planet Earth is totally ridiculous. So, what can you do? I have spent time educating myself about what's really going on. Ten years ago, I sent healing energy to everybody and everything in this world. Governments, heads of state, UN meetings, whole nations, honestly, the whole lot. I could name any world leader. I knew what was going on in politics, and the economy. What a complete and utter waste of time. Big ego or complete idiot, still not sure, the same thing really. I think big, but you see that was the problem. I was thinking and worrying. You can't win by worrying. You just add and create more worry for the world. You have no power to create a good future if you constantly worry and create worry. The power you need is to trust that solutions will be found to create a positive future in your imagination. A good place to start is to see all of humanity living without poverty and war.

At this moment in time, if I do find out that something 'negative' may happen, I construct a Medicine Wheel and ask for a peaceful solution. I make a wish in my Medicine Wheel. Every single wish that I have asked for has always been granted, big or small. This is a good way to help heal this world. Construct a Medicine Wheel. Now, I live in my imagination, creating a life worth living. I start my day with fun wrestling my Grizzly Bear. Now, that's quite an achievement. As long as you don't live near real Grizzly Bears you should be fine.

Learn to play again, but don't go all moody and start saying: My Dolphin has no fins and my Coyote said she hates me. I can't catch my crazy Grizzly Bear and my Elk is in a bad mood and keeps tutting at me. *Just relax*. Come on, it is a little bit funny. Learn to laugh about it, don't take anything seriously anymore. There really is no point.

All you need to realize is that you are the All Powerful Creator. This is your Universe. Just know you can stand in the middle of your Medicine Wheel, call the 36 Power animals in at the same time and declare them all fit and well, in an instant. Get it? Why make life hard. It's easy, when you know how. Here is a way to call in your Power Animals.

The Planet Earth Medicine Wheel is a place in my imagination. I imagine walking through a lush, bright green forest. I come to a large clearing ahead of me. I imagine there is a Medicine Wheel, consisting of twelve tall clear quartz crystals, and a large turquoise solid crystal rock in the middle, with a small violet flamed fire burning brightly with white sage at the base.

At each of the four directions are tall elegant trees, Oak, Cedar, Pine and Maple. I stand with my creator Power Animal, a Lioness. I call to all the plants, animals, crystals and all of humanity to be here now, to share in this healing Medicine Wheel, to allow in love, gratitude and peace to all of the Universe, the Stars and the Planets, Great Spirit, Great Mystery and the Great Void.

I imagine standing in the centre with a golden contract in my hand. I now ask all 36 Power Animals to acknowledge this contract. I call in the following Power Animals in this order: Golden Eagle, Coyote, Grizzly Bear, White Buffalo, Creator *(can be any animal you wish, however, I recommend a Lion/Lioness)*, Snow Goose, Otter, Cougar, Red Hawk, Beaver, Deer, Woodpecker, Sturgeon, Brown Bear, Raven, Snake, Elk, Tortoise, Lizard, Loon, Turtle, Frog, Thunderbird *(magical Native American creature)*, Butterfly, Hummingbird, Owl, Firefly, Rabbit, Salmon, Wolf, Whale, Mouse, Ant, Raccoon, Earthworm and Dolphin.

Whales, Dolphins, Salmon and Sturgeon can all be in the Medicine Wheel, it's a magical dimension. Feel free to create an ocean, beside your Medicine Wheel if you want, I have them floating in the air.

Tell them, you're the boss. They will all giggle at you. Then you have got it. It's up to you, it has always been up to you. This is how to love yourself and if you wish attract a True Love. If you are having a problem, you're worrying again. Stop it! Most people had a teddy bear when they were a small child. Go and befriend your Brown Bear *(your ability to experience joy and pleasure)*. Or chase your Deer *(your ability to take action)* around for a bit. In your imagination, leap around in the air, or do a double back flip! Be silly.

If you want True Love, spend some time and play with your Wolf. Hug it. Ask it to be beside you, day and night. You will get a partner to be with you through life. Most people's Wolves are covered in bandages and limping. Give your Wolf some hands-on healing. Imagine pale pink and gold mist entering the heart area. Cover the Wolf in gold and copper healing glitter. See your Wolf become healthy, strong and fluffy. Go with your Wolf to visit a mountain at night. Lay down to watch the night stars in the sky and make a wish on a shooting star. Wish for True Love. Be gentle with your Wolf, be gentle with yourself. If you want to, find a photograph of a Wolf and carry it around with you. This is called a totem. Use other photographs to help make a complete Medicine Wheel in your home or garden. You can also draw or paint a picture, make or buy a toy Wolf, or any other animal to represent the part of your soul that you wish to work with.

Please note your Power Animals should be the same sex as you. You can figure out how to tell a female coyote from a male one. Just kidding! You can just tell. Ask if you are unsure. Power Animals always have to tell you the truth. For example, if you are female, and you call your coyote and a male coyote arrives, please send it into the violet mist. This is an over-bearing father or ex-lover. Then ask for your female coyote to appear. She will be very happy, finally, as you got rid of the bully. Obviously, men need to release any female Power Animals in exactly the same way. This usually only happens with Coyotes *(your emotional self)* and Wolves *(your romantic self)*. Nevertheless, you never know!

Since there are obviously more animals than the ones covered by Sun Bear's Medicine Wheel, any animal in the world can be your Power Animal. There is no limit on how many Power Animals you have. I have a herd of Horses *(work)* and pods of Humpback and Killer Whales *(experience)* and a huge colourful Butterfly for telepathy and speaking with Great Spirit.

The first Power Animal I ever saw was a rather battered, but beautiful, Lioness. She turned up in a horrible state. She had many injuries. I gave her so much love. She now accompanies me whenever I call her. She is very big, about twice the size of a normal Lioness. The Lion families are the strongest spiritual protection on Planet Earth at this time. I personally, want everyone to have a Lion or Lioness as a Creator Power Animal. Call it into your Medicine Wheel.

It is your Ultimate Protection.

I dare you to fun wrestle your Lion/Lioness. It's a very interesting experience! The more time spent in the Medicine Wheel, the more time you are spending healing and loving yourself, Planet Earth, All Her Relations and ultimately this entire Universe. The time is now. Become the *TRUE ELITE* of this world.

Planet Earth is in a serious mood because, we the humans are in a serious mood, which means life on this planet will get serious. We do not want this. We need to lighten up fast. We need to cheer up. She wants us humans to cheer up. Remember, we are the co-creators!

Building a Medicine Wheel

At first, I really complicated this simple procedure. So, my advice is to know that. To make a Medicine Wheel, place five rocks or crystals in a circle while calling in the Spirit Keeper Power Animals in the following order. Start in the East, place a stone and call to Golden Eagle, in the South call Coyote, the West is for Grizzly Bear, and the North is for White Buffalo. Place the last stone in the Centre for Creator, this can represent any animal, that's all there is to it, anyone can build and use a real Medicine Wheel.

This is Magic. Pure Magic. Pure Love. Pure Nature. They are all the same. The word magic has had some bad press. Magic, love or nature, these terms all represent the same energy. I will explain.

When you make a Medicine Wheel, either physically or

in your imagination, you tap back into this immense ancient magical and sacred power. Connecting to this power is how you can heal your soul, find True Love for yourself and create a life worth living.

What is your imagination? I believe your imagination can be a vision you hold in your mind, to create what you desire. Your imagination is actually a sacred place to work on yourself. It is your personal magical dimension, where everything is possible. I also believe you can create a healing space and work on yourself by using a personal magical declaration, or an intention.

Some people are too mentally stressed to hold a vision long enough for working on themselves. The solution is to build a real Medicine Wheel, and work with Golden Eagle to heal your mental stress. Then you will be able to hold a vision and work with your imagination. Close your eyes now, and imagine opening your front door. Yes, it's easy. Now imagine a beautiful Grizzly Bear standing right beside you, there it is. See, it's easy. It's called using your imagination. Do not complicate this, just practice.

A Medicine Wheel can be an access point to communicate with the Wisdom of the Soul. A place to connect to Power Animals, Mountains, Oceans, Trees, Plants, Herbs and Crystals. The simple Medicine Wheel needs activating. Which means you will need at least five small or large stones, crystals, or anything you wish to use from nature. If you really want your life back on track, spend time making a full 36 stone Medicine Wheel. Speak to every part of your soul, all 36 Power Animals. Introduce yourself to all of them. Great healing will occur. Work either in your imagination or you can physically construct a Medicine Wheel in your home or garden.

Gather the stones in a sacred manner, asking permission before taking any thing from nature. Make sure that any disturbance of plant and animal life, including insect life, is avoided as far as possible. The creation of the sacred Medicine Wheel is a conscious process.

Find a clear area to build your Medicine Wheel. Light some White Sage or Sweet Grass, any incense is fine, to purify and to bless the area and the items from nature you will be using. Ask the Spirit of Sage to bless the Medicine Wheel and items. If you have no sage, just use your imagination to see the Medicine Wheel items and space being purified with lots of imaginary sage smoke. Make a small offering to the Medicine Wheel. It can be any food you like, a strand of your hair or sea salt, traditionally cornmeal or tobacco would be used. Just place the offering on the Creator position. You may place an offering on a single position or on every position. Once built, always enter your medicine wheel from the South, the one and only rule of the Medicine wheel. Sit anywhere inside and speak out your declaration. This is your guarantee, to be able to heal the entire journey of the soul, to use magic and love again, to find True Love for yourself.

When you build a permanent Medicine Wheel in your home or garden, it becomes a very peaceful healing place to sit in or by. Anyone can sit in your Medicine Wheel. It is a statement of honour to Planet Earth and All Her Relations, which also means all of humanity. It automatically sends healing to rebalance everything in this Universe.

You can read, speak or visualize the following as an example of how to activate either a Medicine Wheel in your imagination, or a real Medicine Wheel. Your Power Animal is the same sex as you. So, obviously if you're a man say "He". Face the direction as you call to each Power Animal:

In the East, *I call in my Golden Eagle. She/he is here to give (state your complete name) powerful healing, to cleanse my mental body. We are now and forever connected by love and respect. I thank Golden Eagle.*

In the South, *I call in my Coyote. She/he is here to give (state your complete name) powerful healing, to cleanse my emotional body. We are now and forever connected by love and respect. I thank Coyote.*

In the West, *I call in my Grizzly Bear. She/he is here to give (state your complete name) powerful healing, to cleanse my spiritual body. We are now and forever connected by love and respect. I thank Grizzly Bear.*

In the North, *I call in my White Buffalo. She/he is here to give (state your complete name) powerful healing, to cleanse my physical body. We are now and forever connected by love and respect. I thank White Buffalo.*

In the Centre, *I call in Great Spirit, my Creator Power Animal. She/he is here to give (state your complete name) powerful healing, to cleanse my soul. We are now and forever connected by love and respect. I thank Great Spirit, my Creator Power Animal.*

A small Medicine Wheel is just as powerful. Think about making a Medicine Wheel for every household member. It may serve as a 'time out' space for children. Ask them to go and talk to their Power Animals to receive healing and peace – much nicer for your children than the famous naughty step policy. Sit there for seven minutes because you're seven! What is that programming all about? If you want your children to behave, correct your own behaviour.

The Medicine Wheel[3]

by Sun Bear and Wabun Wind

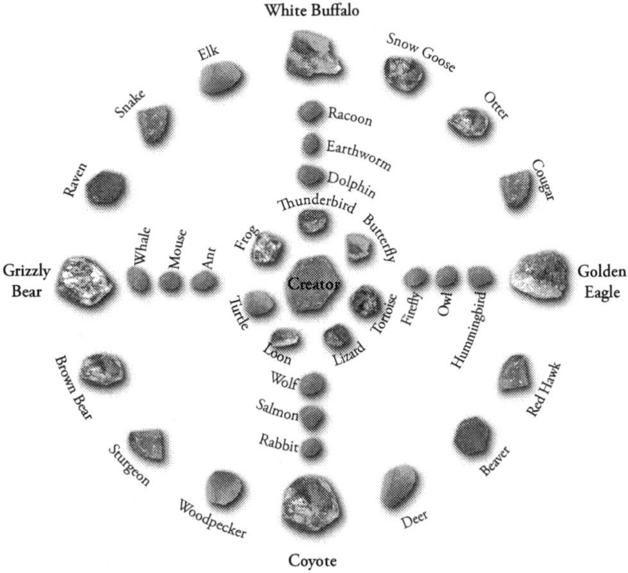

3 This material is from 'The Medicine Wheel: Earth Astrology' by Sun Bear and Wabun Wind, published by Simon and Schuster, New York, 1980, and available from your favourite book seller or online from www.wabunwind.com, The material is used with permission of the author.

The Spirit Keepers

The four Spirit Keeper Animals represent the four Cardinal directions. The first is placed in the East. The Creator is at the centre of the circle:

Golden Eagle	*The East*	Mental self
Coyote	*The South*	Emotional self
Grizzly Bear	*The West*	Spiritual self
White Buffalo	*The North*	Physical self
Any Animal	*Creator*	Connection to Great Spirit

The Twelve Moons

North to East, in a clockwise order of the twelve moons:

Snow Goose	*Capricorn*	Create the life you desire
Otter	*Aquarius*	Learn to relax and be playful
Cougar	*Pisces*	Empowering your inner self
Red Hawk	*Aries*	Learn optimism
Beaver	*Taurus*	Learn balance
Deer	*Gemini*	The ability to take action
Woodpecker	*Cancer*	The ability to be courageous
Sturgeon	*Leo*	Access your sexuality
Brown Bear	*Virgo*	Learn to experience pleasure
Raven	*Libra*	Learn to accept yourself
Snake	*Scorpio*	Learn to transform yourself
Elk	*Sagittarius*	Learn self responsibility

The Inner Circle

Continuing in a clockwise direction, the first position is slightly to the South of East:

Tortoise	*Mother Earth*	Be a universal human being
Lizard	*Father Sun*	Increase personal energy
Loon	*Grandmother Moon*	Create something new
Turtle	*Element of Earth*	Learn to care for all
Frog	*Element of Water*	Learn about addictions
Thunderbird	*Element of Fire*	Learn to be kind to all
Butterfly	*Element of Air*	Honour the coming changes

The Spirit Pathways

The Four Spirit Pathways lead from the Spirit Keeper Animals to the centre:

In the East (Golden Eagle)

Hummingbird	Owl	Firefly
Learn gracefulness	*Learn how to love*	*Find the light within*

In the South (Coyote)

Rabbit	Salmon	Wolf
Heal your inner child	*Learn to trust life*	*How to find true love*

In the West (Grizzly Bear)

Whale	Mouse	Ant
Honour your life	*Reorganise your life*	*Find your strength*

In the North (White Buffalo)

Raccoon	Earthworm	Dolphin
Be truthful	*Rejuvenate yourself*	*Learn to be peaceful*

Golden Eagle

Mental Self

Ask Golden Eagle to help with clearing and centring the mind, by healing and releasing stress and old thought patterns that no longer serve you. Create a new positive mental attitude.

Coyote

Emotional Self

Ask Coyote to help with clearing and releasing old emotional responses from the past that stop you being a strong compassionate and loving person. Create a new positive emotional self.

Grizzly Bear

Spiritual Self

Ask Grizzly Bear to help with releasing limited religious beliefs learnt in past lives or in this life, that are preventing you from truly loving yourself. Create a new humane spiritual identity.

White Buffalo

Physical Self

Ask White Buffalo to help with releasing old physical ailments and injuries from the physical body. Ask for healing and restoring your life force energy. Create a new healthy and strong physical body.

Creator

Your connection to Great Spirit

Ask your Power Animal to connect you to Great Spirit. Honour and give thanks for your life, your family and friends. To make you a 'Great Spirit' so you can help yourself and others find happiness.

Snow Goose

Create the life you desire

Ask Snow Goose to help you release any beliefs that prevent you from creating abundance. Ask for healing energy to return your creative abilities. Create a life worth living.

Otter

Learn to relax and be playful

Ask Otter to help you release limiting thoughts and sad emotions that prevent you from experiencing joy in your life. Ask Otter to show you how to relax and be playful. Create a life you enjoy.

Cougar

Empowering your inner self

Ask cougar to help with personal boundaries. To send healing to clear all self doubt. To be able to stand up for yourself, others, Planet Earth and All Her Relations. Create and exhibit inner strength.

Red Hawk

Learn optimism

Ask Red Hawk to clear all negative energy. To teach you to be open to new ideas and help from others. Ask to be given healing for insight and adaptability. Create your life in an optimistic and positive way.

Beaver

Learn balance

Ask Beaver to cleanse and clear any feelings of lack of self worth and lack of self love. Ask to learn how to remain balanced and stable. To allow in affection and healing. To create a balanced life.

Deer

The ability to take action

Ask Deer to clear and cleanse all feelings of lethargy. To ask for healing to be given to start to create the plans and ideas that you want to manifest in your life. To activate your life from within.

Woodpecker

The ability to be courageous

Ask woodpecker to help you find the courage to start to love yourself again. Ask for healing for letting go of old ways that keep you in fear. Find the courage to create a life worth living.

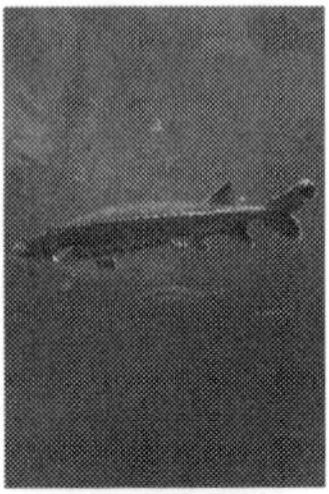

Sturgeon

Access your sexuality

Ask Sturgeon to release old sexual beliefs that stop you experiencing and enjoying a healthy and loving sexual relationship. Ask for healing to be given to let go of past love affairs. Create a new sexual identity.

Brown Bear

Learn to experience pleasure

Ask Brown Bear to help you release any thoughts or feelings of depression. Ask to send healing to help experience new pleasure and love. Create a life full of pleasure and love.

Raven

Learn to accept yourself

Ask Raven to help you to heal your shadow. To accept and understand your past. To let go of judgement and replace with compassion for yourself and others. Become a compassionate human being.

Snake

Learn to transform yourself

Ask Snake to help you let go of all limiting attitudes about yourself that prevent you from attaining your goals. Ask for healing to transform your self image. Manifest the energy to create the life you desire.

Elk

Learn self responsibilty

Ask Elk to help you release the habit of blaming others. Ask for healing to realise that the power to change your life begins with taking full responsibilty for all your life experiences.

Tortoise

Be a universal human being

Ask Tortoise to clear any feelings of inadequacy. Ask for healing to accept how amazing and magical humans truly are. Find your true power within. Become a magical universal human being.

Lizard

Increase personal energy

Ask Lizard to help you learn to increase your personal energy. Ask for healing to clear physical tiredness. Renew yourself by eating healthy natural food. Create more sacred energy by being in nature.

Loon

Create something new

Ask the Loon to help wash away the old. Ask for healing with new projects and creations. Use your ability to work with the cycles of the moon. Create and discover the newness of life. Learn to live again.

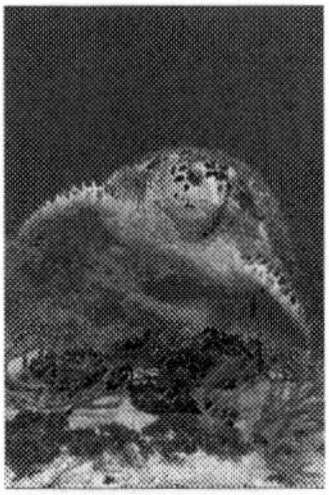

Turtle

Learn to care for all life

Ask turtle to help you to learn how to care for yourself. Ask for healing energy to be sent to yourself and all that dwells in this beautiful world. Create a caring attitude, which creates a caring world.

frog

Learn about addictions

Ask Frog to wash away your unwanted addictions and old modes of behaviour. Ask for healing to clear old emotions and thoughts that keep you stuck in old addictive cycles. Dare to be addiction free.

Thunderbird

Learn to be kind to all

Ask Thunderbird to teach you how to be in service to others, by letting go of self importance. Ask for help to become a kind and loving human being. Create a kind and loving attitude towards all.

Butterfly

Honour the coming changes

Ask Butterfly for wisdom and the courage to welcome the changes needed to create a life worth living. Accept healing and guidance to become more of who you really are. Create and welcome change.

Hummingbird

Learn gracefulness

Ask Hummingbird to draw out the old wounds from your life experience. Ask for healing to strengthen your resolve by creating a better world for yourself and others. Heal this life and world.

Owl

Learn how to love

Ask Owl to show you both sides of the story, so you can find love and compassion for everyone. Learn to be a non-judgmental human being. Be everyone's confidant. Stay neutral. Be love.

Firefly

Find the light within

Ask Firefly to bring light to the darkest aspects of your being. Ask for healing to clear the fears you still hold. Finding the light within requires you to stop recreating all your fears. Cultivate fearlessness.

Rabbit

Heal the child within

Ask Rabbit to show you how to connect to your inner child. Ask for healing to be given to your inappropriate automatic emotional responses, so you can grow up. Heal and love your inner child.

Salmon

Learn to trust life

Ask Salmon to show you how to learn to trust yourself and your ability to create a life worth living. Ask for guidance and wisdom so you can learn to trust that your life is in safe hands, your own.

Wolf

How to find true love

Ask wolf to heal all doubts that stop you finding true love for yourself. Ask for healing to help you create a life with your one true love. Create a path to your true love, by loving yourself unconditionally.

Whale

Honour your life

Ask Whale to help you acknowledge how experienced you really are at loving yourself. Ask for healing for your self image. Create a good feeling for yourself. Honour your life so far.

Mouse

Reorganise your life

Ask Mouse to show you what needs reorganising in your life. Throw away the old, to make space for the new. Cultivate good habits and learn what is good for your life. Create skills to organise your life.

Ant

Find your strength

Ask Ant to show you all your strengths and all your weaknesses. Ask for healing to be given to your weaknesses and learn to acknowledge and honour your strengths. Create balance for yourself. Be real.

Racoon

Be truthful

Ask Racoon to give you the courage to always speak your truth. To take off your mask and be comfortable with who you are. Always speak with kindness and gentleness and see your world become real.

Earthworm

Rejuvenate yourself

Ask Earthworm to show you how thoughts and feelings effect your outward appearance and health. Ask for awareness of how you really think and feel about your physical image. Create and renew yourself.

Dolphin

Learn to be peaceful

Ask Dolphin to heal all thoughts of frustration. Ask to have a better understanding of what you are adding to this world. Learn to trust yourself again. Learn to let go and create peaceful solutions.

Nine

Medicine Wheel Meditations

Golden Eagle Meditation

Connect with your Golden Eagle, the Spirit Keeper of the East, where the sun rises. Golden Eagle represents new creations or your wishes. It also represents the mind and your mental state.

Using just your imagination, ask your Golden Eagle to bless your mind and cleanse all programming and preconditioning that you no longer need to have in your life. Imagine it leaving and going up into a large, very bright star, way above your head, in the sky. Ask to have wisdom and understanding sent back. Now feel your head lighten.

Go and make friends with your Golden Eagle, see it grow very big, glowing in golden light and get onto its back and go fly across the entire beautiful multi-coloured galaxy, passing the stars and the planets. Leave this world and find your own sacred space in this beautiful Universe. Be free from everybody and everything, be with SELF. Be at one with your Golden Eagle. Be at one with your mind. Be a peace. Thank Golden Eagle and return to the present.

Coyote Meditation

Connect to your Coyote, the Spirit Keeper of the South, where the sun is highest in the sky. It represents your present feelings and your emotional body. Ask Coyote to help clear all your old emotions and cleanse all your emotional responses that you are generationally programmed with, and preconditioning that you no longer need to have in your life. Imagine them leaving and going up into a large, very bright star, way above your head, in the sky.

Send all your old emotional patterns, old feelings and responses, up out of your being. Send them up to the bright star, representing Great Spirit. Now feel your heart lighten and smile.

Make friends with your Coyote. See your Coyote start to glow an amazing silver colour, climb on his back and visit the sacred turquoise waterfall. Enter the pool of turquoise water and let it cleanse your emotional body. Feel the water repairing your DNA. Your emotional and feeling body begins to vibrate, and for a moment, you become invisible, and are able to let go of every single feeling and emotion you have ever had throughout all your Past lives. Return to your original state of being – an Original Divine Soul. Be at one with your Soul. Thank Coyote and return to the present moment.

Grizzly Bear Meditation

Connect to your Grizzly Bear, the Spirit Keeper of the West, where the sun sets in the sky. It represents your spiritual self, your belief system that you adopted in this lifetime. Ask Grizzly Bear to help clear old, out-dated belief systems that no longer serve you. See all your old belief patterns floating up and out of your entire being to Great Spirit. Feel your heart relax and lighten as you release all the old beliefs held there.

Now, go back in time with Grizzly Bear, many tens of thousands of years ago. Imagine walking down a time line into a beautiful mountain range. Notice the evening sun setting. See a large cave entrance, this is the Divine Bear cave. A place to receive spiritual healing. Request a shamanic healing treatment and allow a shaman to come and purify your spiritual self of all things that hold you back from being a truly creative spiritual being. Stay as long as you like, filling your entire being with spiritual wisdom. Finish by asking the Grizzly Bear to home with you. Thank your Grizzly Bear, and ask your inner being to ground yourself fully in the present.

White Buffalo Meditation

Connect to your White Buffalo, the Spirit Keeper of the North, where it is night and the stars are high in the sky. Your. White Buffalo represents the future and your physical body. Ask White Buffalo to bless your body and your future and to release all your physical illnesses or regular ailments *(aches and pains, and old injuries)*.

Imagine all your health problems leaving your body, mind and aura – your entire being – send it up to the bright star that represents Great Spirit, Great Mystery and the Great

Void. Ask to be sent back wisdom and understanding. Now feel your entire body lighten.

Go and make friends with your White Buffalo, see it grow very big, glowing in golden light. Get onto its back and go running across the plains to most favourite place in the world. Talk to White Buffalo about helping you create the future you desire. What are your future plans? What are you going to create? Why not include the whole of humanity in your future plans? Help steer us all in the best direction. We only have each other, it's best we all stick together. Be a good example. Be masterful about your future. Be wise too! What is best for everyone should be your stand point. We are all equal. We are all one, actually. Be the spirit of the sacred White Buffalo. Be its medicine.

Creator Meditation

Connect with your Spirit Keeper representing Creator. This can be any animal. My favourite is the Lion/Lioness, representing the highest spiritual protection. It is your connection to Great Spirit, Great Mystery and the Great Void. Ask this Power Animal to bless your Life.

Using just your imagination, start to walk towards a large waterhole in the deepest part of Africa. See a large group of Lions and Lionesses laying around in the Sun. Call over and ask your Power Animal to reveal itself. You will see one of the Lions or Lionesses get up and come towards you. It will probably walk around you three times as a ceremony of bonding. As it walks around you, it is healing you, first your aura, then your body and finally your Soul.

Imagine releasing all your old and tired energy up and out of your entire being - your body, mind and aura. Release all your yesterdays, live in the present. Become good friends with your Creator Power Animal. Become good friends with Great Spirit. Be a Great Spirit

Uniting all the Tribes

In your imagination you can visit the sacred World Peace Medicine Wheel to meet with Sun Bear who is in spirit. The Chief of the Bear Tribe's vision is to unite all people of this world and to help preserve Planet Earth for future generations to come. You can join the Bear Tribe if you ask. In your imagination, walk into an area where the massive redwood trees of California stand in a large circle, a living World Peace Medicine Wheel.

Always enter the Medicine Wheel from the South. This is the one and only rule to Medicine Wheels. This is where your Coyote and emotions are, and you must be able to heal all of your old emotions, as this is what needs to be healed. Imagine your Golden Eagle, Coyote, Grizzly Bear and White Buffalo accompanying you inside the Medicine Wheel. Also, always call to your Creator Power Animal.

Just wait patiently for Sun Bear. He will appear and probably give you an almighty hug. Do not be surprised if he comes as a huge Grizzly Bear. Sit down with him and tell him all your worries and then send them up to Great Spirit. Remember, Great Spirit is a bright star above your head. Push all your worries up into the star. Use this technique daily to clear your energy field. It is a very simple and powerful way of letting go of the old you, the one that blames others by moaning and complaining. Let her/him go please! Do this as often as you need to. Learn to clear your thinking mind, your body and your aura.

While you are still in the World Peace Medicine Wheel, you may request healing from Great Spirit and Sun Bear. Imagine a healing table and go and lay down on the table and accept a healing treatment from Sun Bear. When you are finished, thank him and Great Spirit. It may be a good time to give thanks to Planet Earth for everything you have ever had from her.

Bear in mind that you are an amazing magical being who is better than any other being in this entire universe when it comes to healing yourself. Only you can truely heal yourself. Open your heart and ask for healing to unite all the peoples of this world.

> ***"The Medicine Wheel is a springboard of power that will allow you to link up with all the energies of the Universe."***
>
> ***Sun Bear, Chief of the Bear Tribe***

Ten

Medicine Wheel Readings

Are you ready to travel with the Medicine Wheel? Remember, we are going to access different parts of your soul. We do this by visiting each Power Animal that represents each part of your soul. There are five aspects to your soul, or five Power Animals to visit, to complete the basic Medicine Wheel Soul Reading.

The first thing you should do is to find out how you are really feeling now. Practice, in your imagination, connecting to the five Power Animals: Golden Eagle *(mental)*; Coyote *(emotional)*; Grizzly Bear *(spiritual)*; White Buffalo *(physical)*; and Creator *(Great Spirit)*. Just wait and see what animal turns up for Creator, or invite a Lion or Lioness.

Watch how your Power Animals are presenting themselves to you. Did they come immediately? How big are they? Do they like you? Try walking around them. Notice them from all angles. They may look fine from the front, but sometimes their back legs are injured. If you are completely unsure, just imagine touching the animal's head and filling them up with violet healing energy. You are giving healing to your present self.

If you are good at visualizing, it may take you a couple of hours. This is how long it takes me, to do a reading for the soul. I know that if you want self-healing enough, you do not have to actually see the Power Animals, just decide they are in front of you and speak to them in your imagination. Or paint them, or sing to them. The Power Animals also communicate on behalf of the all the animals. The animals want the humans to cheer up, they still love us. They are eager to help us, we should be grateful. They have not lost faith in us, this is a good sign.

Heal Your Present Pain

I once impressed a top psychiatrist who wanted to know what I had said to Howard *(not his real name)*. The psychiatrist had been counselling him three times a week for many years. However, two hours in a Medicine Wheel and he was a changed man. This man was very upset about a former girlfriend who had died. I invited her to his Medicine Wheel. He got a chance to speak with her, it was a deeply moving experience for him. After that, I explained that he needed to let go of his emotional upset with regard to this girlfriend. If she is in spirit, she was not meant to be with him in this life. He finally found peace, he was able to live in the present. He started dating again.

You don't need anyone to do this for you, you can do this in your Medicine Wheel. Take the chance to say what you have not been able to say. Listen to what they have to say too. However, do this only once, if they are in spirit. When you are finished, always thank them for coming. Then see them walk into violet healing mist and vanish. Next, imagine Great Spirit as a very bright shining star above your head, way up high in the night sky. Imagine releasing all your thoughts and feelings, by sending them up to Great Spirit. This helps by clearing your old emotions and keeps your energy field clear. Your energy field is your mind, body and aura. Live in the present moment. This is where your true power is. Be present. Be here now.

If you have unresolved hurt and upset about a living person, then in your imagination invite them into your Medicine Wheel and speak honestly to them about how you are feeling. Then send all your feelings to Great Spirit *(the star above)* and see them walk into violet healing mist and vanish. Let it go, and move on. Be present. This is very important.

Some people are very angry and bitter, and are always talking in a bad way about others. I inform them that they are really talking about themselves. Because that mind of theirs is listening and creating all that bitterness, again and again. Stop this immediately. Your external world is made by you, if you don't like what is happening in your world, correct your own behaviour, from within. Be kind to everyone, but overall, be kind to yourself. You only see yourself in this life through others. Do not add aggression and bitterness to this world, there is plenty here already! It takes at least two people to have an argument. Stay silent and be peaceful. Send your own stress up to Great Spirit and ask for wisdom to be returned to you, so that you can understand and stop creating these stressful situations in the first place.

Accessing a Past Life

A Medicine Wheel is a simple Time Machine, a sacred place to travel backwards or forwards in time to communicate with your former selves *(past lives)* and future potential self, for this current life. It is also possible to access your next incarnation, it just depends how adventurous you are.

If you wish to access a past life, just create a beautiful Medicine Wheel in your imagination. First, call for your Creator Power Animal to arrive, and then call a former self who can give you the greatest healing at this time. If you wait, a former self will arrive. Treat all former selves with great respect and honour, regardless of how they look and act. Realize that this spirit has come to help you, and hopefully you can help this former self. Some former selves just want to sit and have a chat, so just listen and if necessary provide a hug. Some former past lives will ask you to travel back in time. Just imagine walking down a time line. Imagine a path stretching out before you. Sometimes if you are going a long way back in time, fly holding hands with your former self. Remember to have some fun! Just observe what you are shown, and know that you are conducting all of this healing in your imagination and have full protection at all times.

When they *(former selves)* first come to the Medicine Wheel, notice, what do they look like? Who are they? Where do they live, and in what time period? How are they feeling? Are they distressed? Remember, in your imagination you have the power to set all things right. Ask them what is the matter? Why have you come to the Medicine Wheel? Do you need my help? How can I help you at this time?

Be aware that your former selves are probably going to do the 'poor me brigade'. This is very common. Be nice. Just don't give them any sympathy. If they are children, call in their mother and father. Use your common sense. Comfort and listen to them. I find former selves are non-aggressive in most cases. If you are confronted by a lot of aggression, snap your fingers in your imagination and turn them into a six year old. They will be much easier to deal with. You're the boss. Pull rank!

Remember this is your universe, you are in charge at all times. You may need to be firm with your former selves at times. You may have been a General with an ego the size of the Empire State Building! Being firm means being in control of the healing.

Many former selves are not aware that you are their future self, so tell them. Most only realize this when you explain that they are constantly being born again without gaining spiritual knowledge, forever stuck in the holding bay of Fake Reincarnation. Tell them you can free their soul in an instant. Each former self can be released, this is very powerful healing. Just send them home into the violet mist and see them vanish into the Divine.

As previously stated, the soul is best viewed as a personal library of all the past lives you have had. These past lives hold much of your power. Reviewing and healing events in past lives can empower and strengthen you in your present life. Just imagine being able to comfort a mother of a former self who lost her child at sea, and they still carry this pain, which is held in your soul. She can come forward for healing. And you, as the healer, have magical and unlimited powers in your imagination. Ask for the lost child's spirit to appear and watch with great love the reunion your soul has been asking for, maybe for centuries. Create the happy endings. Imagine magically healing an eleven-year-old boy with an appalling disfigurement of the face, that happened in Delhi, India in 1882, when he fell into a pit. What was I thinking in that life? Imagine healing yourself when you fled Tibet with the current Dalai Lama, but got sick on the way to India and died, away from your spiritual homeland.

I was actually a steward for the current Dalai Lama, a few years ago at Alexandra Palace. I had to stand about 5 feet from him for many hours, and he kept staring at me. I knew we had been childhood friends. I think he knew it too! I also drew massive Tibetan healing symbols all over the hall in my imagination. He was looking at the ceiling, then at me, and then back at the ceiling. I thought, "Oops! He knows! I hope he doesn't mind!"

Some past lives are a little sad, like when I was conscripted into World War I, having to kill many people, having that sorrow and despair in my soul. Similarly, you may not have been able to forgive yourself on some level deep inside. So, heal this sadness. These are some of my healed past lives.

I understand we all need to make a big leap in consciousness, so, maybe we can heal yesterday, which heals today and heals the future, which in turn will heal this world. I truly believe we have the potential to be our greatest self now. Go and love all of yourself, meaning love all parts of your soul. It is easy and you can make it a good experience. Be the *TRUE ELITE*. Claim and find your power within, True Love for your True Self.

Remember, you have the ability of an All Powerful Creator to heal and solve every problem, as you are not restricted by time and space or magical abilities. Plus, you have Power Animals and Love on your side. Be a God or Goddess of Love.

You may ask, "How will I know if these are really my past lives?" And I say, do this only once. You will feel it without a question, or doubt, as you feel the tears running down your face. It's called the tear test. You will cry with happiness.

You create a space where the pain of your soul can get the exact healing it needs instantly. No, *'poor me brigade'.* It is past, heal it, sort it and then, very importantly, let it all go. Flood your Medicine Wheel, the Power Animals, former selves and your current self with violet and pale pink mist. Pale pink is the colour of unconditional love. Have unconditional love for yourself.

Past Life Healing

I had a school friend, a young man, who once had a very bad heart condition which was causing him to black out all the time. There was no hope of a cure. What had he been doing in a past life?

In my imagination, we travelled back in time and discovered he was once an arrogant Spanish bull fighter. He had spent many years cutting out the hearts of the Bulls, while they were still alive! Bulls represent White Buffalo *(your physical self)*, which in turn means your physical body, your health, as well as your future.

We called, in his imagination, to the Medicine Wheel all the Bulls he had abused in spirit form, one by one. He apologized, and gave back all the physical hearts. He promised that he would never do it again. He asked for their forgiveness. It was granted, and the next thing we knew, a surgical doctor in the USA had invented a device to cure his heart condition. This man is now very healthy.

Understand, you can do wonders in your imagination. This man suffered for 37 years until he did this Medicine Wheel past life therapy healing session. He is very wealthy, so money was never the issue. He got the cure because he healed himself on a soul level and the world responded with a miracle to heal him. Life is truly wonderful.

You can correct all your crimes against others. You can give yourself another chance. Just take a look around you, most people are depressed and sad. Most people need to give themselves another chance to learn to love themselves again.

We can easily become stuck in a rut. Worrying and creating negative thoughts, which manifest into negative lives. However, once we learn to truley love ourselves again, we automatically create a life worth living. Learn to love again and using your imagination create a different, softer, energy to heal this world.

Mass Past Life Healing Meditation

You can create a sacred Medicine Wheel to do a Mass Past Life Healing. Please take the time to imagine standing in your Medicine Wheel, somewhere beautiful in nature. Visualise and call in your Creator Power Animal and your four main Spirit Keepers, Golden Eagle, Coyote, Grizzly Bear and White Buffalo. Next, in your imagination call to the Medicine Wheel every past life, all your former selves. You will start to see the many wonderful souls slowly walking towards the sacred Medicine Wheel.

You will have a large crowd of many men, women and children of different nationalities, in different clothing, representing different religious backgrounds from different times. This is also a quick way to let go of conditioned prejudices that separate us. Whether one is a Chinese Buddhist, Malay Muslim, French Roman Catholic or Australian Aboriginal, we are all the same, really. We are magical eternal souls that live for a short time in different bodies, in different places and at different times. These collective soul experiences make you a magical universal human being.

If you want, you can ask them to stand in groups of the similar types of vocation. Do you know how many times I have been a monk? Do you know how many times as a soldier, that my life ended prematurely on the battlefield in the name of the King, Chief or some other useless villain?

Do you know how many times I have been a shaman, farmer, midwife or cook? What has happened to you? Who have you been? You need to find out so you can acknowledge who you really are. You can also ask your past lives to show you what you have created with your time on Planet Earth.

Have you built houses, schools, cathedrals, pyramids or ancient temples? Have you ever invented something amazing and life transforming? Have you ever sailed across an ocean, or trekked across a mountain range? Have you ever lived in an ancient forest, cave or tribe? Have you ever been a teacher, leader or Chief? Did you perfect the art of drawing, painting, dancing or singing? Did you perfect the art of shamanism with Trees, Herbs, Plants, Crystals? Have you ever been Native American, or an African or Japanese? How many different languages have you spoken in your past lives? How many different continents have you lived on? Have you lived over 20,000 years ago or in the 1600's or 1800's.

You can ask for all your skills to be returned to you, immediately. This is your right. It has been included in your Golden Soul Contract, that I hope you signed! The questions are endless. Who are you? What have you accomplished, and what have you done in your past lives? Is it still affecting this life?

After I had trained in basic year one, Zen Shiatsu, I had the opportunity of treating many advanced Zen Shiatsu teachers that noticed I was applying advanced techniques, naturally, without having taken the advanced training. This is because, at the age of 25, I was able to gently go into a state of heightened awareness to access my skills and knowledge from my past life when I was an expert Zen Shiatsu Doctor hundreds of years ago. I just mentally stepped aside and let my hands work, how and where they wanted.

Your soul's inner intelligence remembers all your life experiences and can help you access the knowledge and skills, automatically. We actually don't need to train in anything, we have done all the training that we will ever need. It is about re-remembering who you really are, a magical universal human being.

The first time I rode a horse was in Africa. I was 10 years old. The riding instructor asked me how long I had been riding. I looked at my watch and replied, "11 minutes." She looked totally amazed, as I naturally started to control and ride the large horse I was sitting on. I accessed this skill, instantly. A great love from the many past lives I had as a horse rider. What are you naturally good at? I wonder why? Don't you ever wonder why?

Release Limiting Vows & Soul Contracts

All medieval monks are required to take a vow of poverty. Imagine still being controlled by vows you spoke or signed, made under very stressful circumstances, due to food shortages 700 years ago. It meant you had to become a monk, or starve to death. So, just in case you spoke any vows, say this aloud, and mean it.

"I now cancel all Vows from any past life that are still affecting this life."

A soul contract is usually made between two or more

souls that agree to often preposterous demands of one another. Imagine two teenagers in love, who are blocked from marriage by their respective families. They declare that they will never be in love again. For many future incarnations, until they learn to love themselves again, they have lives that are without love. It is common to go for monk/nun lives, as they have no interest in loving another human being. Eventually they may find each other, in the same life, at the same time, many lives later. They get married, and end up hating each other! Great! Can you see how lost your soul can become, because you made certain choices as a spoiled teenager a few hundred years ago? I did this! This choice resulted in my being a monk for many lives. So, just in case you made any silly soul contracts, just say this aloud, and mean it.

"I now cancel all Soul Contracts from any past life that are still affecting this life."

When people tell me that they believe they will never find love, I laugh and tell them, "You have known great love many hundreds of times." Remember, every life brings love, friendships and big adventures. I have focused on the shadow side of our soul because this is what needs healing. It is important that you say this out loud, and mean it.

"I now ask that all my Past lives receive the healing and love necessary to make a positive powerful healing impact on this life."

Merging All Your Past Lives Meditation

You can ask all your past lives to merge into one Human

Being of Light inside your Medicine Wheel. Try this:

Imagine standing in your Medicine Wheel. Please take the time to visualise and call in your Creator Power Animal and your four main Spirit Keepers, Golden Eagle, Coyote, Grizzly Bear and White Buffalo.

Imagine all your past lives merged into one Human Being standing in front of you.

Create golden light coming out of your hands and see this healing energy fill up the Human Being of Light, from the feet to the heart area.

Next, see the golden light fill the area from the heart to the top of the head, creating an entire golden light being radiating pure golden light as bright as the sun.

Then walk into this Golden Being of Light. To become one with all your past lives, your former selves.

In your imagination, call back the following soul qualities that you have scattered. Call back your magical healing abilities, all of your past spiritual wisdom, any shamanic skills, talents and abilities that could be of use in this lifetime, now. Stay holding this image for a minute and absorb the Golden Light.

Then step out of the Golden Being of Light and send the Golden Being of Light into the violet healing mist, back to the Divine. Finish the process by seeing yourself in your imagination, sitting on the ground in your Medicine Wheel. To bring you back to the present time use the following grounding ceremony.

Grounding Ceremony

Call the element of Fire to come as a Violet Flame to encircle the entire Medicine Wheel, inside as well. Be the Violet Flame. Ask Fire to always be a friend.

Call the element of Water to come as Rain. Hear and feel the raindrops falling heavily all around you. Feel the water cleansing your mind, body and soul. Ask Water to always be a friend.

Call the element of Air to come as the Great Winds and Dancing Storms, gently drying you. Feel the power of the Great wind and Dancing Storms as it encircles your mind, body and soul with love. Ask Air to always be a friend.

Call the element of Earth by placing your hands palms down onto the ground. Connect your soul with the souls of Planet Earth and All Her Relations. Be at one.

Call the element of Love to come as Great Spirit to send down pale green mist that enters and expands your heart chakra. Ask to receive healing from the Plants, Herbs, Flowers and Trees. Ask the Plant Kingdom to always be your friend.

After a Medicine Wheel healing, do not talk about it to anyone for at least three days. This allows a clean disconnection and helps seal the healing without anyone else's energy or opinion added. In six weeks time, you will start to notice that you are skipping down the road, smiling and feeling lighter. We all have a deep pain from our past lives that needs healing. You are accepting who you have really been. You are integrating your shadow self, your dark side. Remember, you are the creator of your life. You have created a place to heal your soul's journey through time.

Go and have a sea salt bath for twenty minutes. Don't think about it: *Let It All Go...* It takes six weeks to clear vows and soul contracts, to heal and merge all your past lives. Be gentle with yourself, and stay calm and grounded.

Future Self Healing

Using a Medicine Wheel to view your future is easy. First, take a look at the Medicine Wheel template, decide which Power Animals can help you with achieving your future goals. Call in your choosen Power Animals and request your future self in five years time comes to the Medicine Wheel. Take a look at your future self. Do you look healthy? Are you happy? What is your future self waiting to tell you?

Remember, it is up to you. No one can create a future for you. I was informed by my future self that I will create large Medicine Healing Fields that span many countries, reorganizing the energetic boundaries of these countries. This will help release old stuck energy, thought forms that create nationalism, as this is counter productive to world peace. I will create strong healing spaces for people to live in peace together, regardless of nationality and race.

I have no desire to receive untruths about myself. I am here to heal myself, which in turn heals Planet Earth. I seek only love and truth. *The truth will set you free*, is my favourite saying. Only by really loving yourself can you truly love another. Seek your own True Love for self and True Love will seek you. This is what we are all really looking for. This is our true soul contract. ***We are love.***

Eleven

Planet Earth Reading

Planet Earth wants to communicate with Her co-creators, us. Why? Because She is in trouble and a little awareness of Her predicament can change the future outcome for Herself and All Her Relations, which includes humankind, and as co-creators, She wishes us to take responsibility and help heal Her soul.

How can you make a difference to this life? By learning the truth about the real state of our planet, which is a reflection of you...*What you have been thinking, feeling and expressing energetically, in short, YOU!*

Mentally she is confused that so-called educated people in the western societies just do not really care about the real state of the environment. The Internet is now full of the correct facts. Nope, nothing much has changed. No real solutions are coming to Her aid.

Emotionally she is worn out, and to be frank, seriously fed up with all the humans. Sound like anyone you know?

Spiritually she is absolutely devastated that you are so unaware of the effects that the energy of the billions of people's greed eating up the future resources of this planet causes...

Devastating humans, animals, insects, sea life, plants, our land, the oceans, the air and every living thing in the universe, including the billions of stars and the rest of the planets. Everything is for sale to the highest bidder. Did you know you could even buy a star? Who said you owned it, to be able to sell the star in the first place?

Physically she is run down. How are you feeling? She is concerned about how unaware the public is about the true state of this planet, the air, water and soil, as pollution levels are off the charts.

Planet Earth's soul is in shock by your total disregard for the truth. Your thinking minds are programmed to service to self, not service to others. Why don't you want to save Planet Earth, and ultimately yourselves?

She wants us to rediscover our ancient knowledge by activating our soul's inner intelligence and connecting to universal wisdom. To remember and know how to respect and take care of our home. She is also shocked. You're all so unaware of your magical co-creating abilities, along with your powerful imaginations, which can put right the problems facing the world at this time. Pure laziness!

These issues are easy to rectify. Yet there seems no one willing to take full responsibility, NOW, for the habitat, and for how we construct our life experience, by realizing we *(humans)* contribute constantly to the current state of the planet – consciously and unconsciously.

As previously mentioned, did you know that everything that you think, say and feel adds energy to this world? What are you thinking, saying and feeling? What are you personally adding to the world at this time? Do you believe everything is doomed? Is this the sort of energy one should be creating and ultimately generating, at this time? Do you have faith in the future of the human race? Do you actually like your fellow man? Do you even like yourself? These issues can be addressed now, at this creative and magical time. Go within and find that True Love for yourself. Find that True Love for Planet Earth and All Her Relations. As we are the ultimate co-creators. This is important.

I wish to share with you the following information I received in *April of 2008*. The Planet Earth Medicine Wheel is a place in my imagination. So, just imagine walking through an ancient beautiful lush green forest. You come to a large clearing ahead of you. Imagine there is a Medicine Wheel, consisting of twelve large, clear quartz crystals, and a large turquoise solid crystal rock in the middle, with a small violet flamed sacred fire burning brightly. There are many flowers, French blue lavender, small white daisies, pale violet orchids, pale pink roses and white roses, all forming an inner circle around the large turquoise crystal. The herb bushes consist of white and purple sage. These are all growing abundantly inside the Medicine Wheel. A small, pure white, baby Snow Owl is sitting in the largest sage bush twittering quietly to her self.

There are four small Japanese bonsai trees, in the four cardinal positions, Oak, Cedar, Pine and Maple. I call in the plants, animals, crystals and all of humanity to be here now, to share in this healing Medicine Wheel, to allow in love and peace to all of the universe, the stars and the planets, especially Planet Earth and All Her Relations.

In the centre, slightly to the south, is a small flowing water fountain made with clear quartz crystals and diamonds. A colourful butterfly, a small green tree frog, a tiny blue bird and a small turtle are sipping the cool clear water and bathing in the fountain together, representing the four elements, to help create magic and love.

My honoured Native American friends in spirit gather in my Medicine Wheel to help heal this world. Chief Sitting Bull in the North, Crazy Horse in the East, Chief Black Elk in the South and Chief Sun Bear is sitting in the West. A small female Lakota Sioux child called Standing Holy *(Sitting Bull's beloved daughter)* is sitting in the centre, representing the children of the past, present and the future.

I am standing with my beautiful Lioness and the Native American called Crazy Horse. The sun is rising, we all sing a Lakota healing song prayer to Planet Earth, All Her Relations and Great Spirit, Great Mystery and the Great Void, from which all of creation comes. Next, I call to Planet Earth's iron crystal heart centre, and the beauty of nature in all her forms, to come to the Medicine Wheel, to help me hear the message that would give Her the greatest healing at this time.

Golden Eagle Needs Healing

I call to Planet Earth's Power Animal, the Spirit Keeper of the East, I call to Golden Eagle, to come and share her wisdom and knowledge. Golden Eagle represents the mental self, or thoughts of the Planet.

I immediately see a very sorry looking brown-feathered Golden Eagle slowly walking towards me. Her feathers are all ruffled up. She is covered in rubbish and crude oil, and she looks and smells horrible. She *(the Golden Eagle)* is swaying from side to side. She wants to throw up. She has allergies *(from chemical poisoning)* and a streaming cold. I magically offer her herbal soap and give her a shower in the crystal fountain with special cleaning herbs to dissolve and clean off the rubbish and oil. I rub her down with a towel, and wrap her up in a very soft blanket and give her a big hug.

I notice there's something wrong with her legs, she is also trying to take deep breaths. She is looking for help. She looks up into the sky and tells me that pollution levels and the air quality are getting worse. She has to think of the future and she is very old. I ask Great Spirit, Great Mystery to come and give healing. Violet healing mist covers Golden Eagle, inside and out. As she breathes in the pure violet colour, she loses her cold and her allergies. This means we will be able, in the near future, to clean up the pollution and toxic chemicals. However, her legs are still unstable. I ask how can I heal your legs and she says, "Tell me that it's okay to save myself." I tell her, "Its okay, go ahead, save yourself."

This means she will do whatever it takes to preserve this planet, who is the mother of us *(on some level)* as we live on Her and She provides for us. She is deeply saddened that it has to come to this high level of destruction of the physical environment. Since we have been doing lots of service to self, we have tipped the scales, now it is Her time for service to self. We have come full circle. Time is running out for the Humans! I thank the Golden Eagle, who has fallen asleep in my arms, and I hand her to Crazy Horse.

Coyote Explains That Planet Earth Has Been Captured

I go stand with Chief Black Elk, and we call to the Spirit Keeper of the South, I call to Coyote to show how Planet Earth is feeling emotionally. I can hear Coyote yelping and snarling. I go and search the forest just outside of my Medicine Wheel. I find Coyote, she is stuck in a man-made barbed-wire trap. Coyote is in great pain. I approach and ask her if I can help free her from the trap. She rolls her eyes at me and says, "Yeah, of course you can." Hmm, I detect a little bit of sarcasm. I manage to release her bloodied paw, she licks it and looks up at me. I ask her if she wants to enter my Medicine Wheel and accept healing for her paw. She agrees, and sits quietly by my violet flame fire. As I heal her paw, Coyote calls to her friend, a beautiful copper brown Mare. The Mare appears suddenly from behind the large trees. Coyote explains that Planet Earth has been captured. Horse represents work. Planet Earth has been turned into a workhorse for the fake elite.

I notice that she is looking directly at me. She is not alone. She has a broken bridle on. I see a group of people standing behind her holding the reins tightly. I see them hanging on for dear life! They are now losing their grip on the reins. They, the fake elite, have also all fallen out of the saddle. The Mare has thrown them all off.

Coyote tells us, "The fake elite that have captured Planet Earth and her resources are deliberately destroying the environment. Just take a look around you. Why can't you see that the world is becoming near impossible to live in, as it becomes an ever-expanding toxic rubbish dump? The fake elite have been controlling pretty much everything on this planet. However, changes are afoot!" Coyote winks at me, so does the Mare. They have a secret they wish to share, "Planet Earth has a Divine Soul rescue plan. She requested help a long time ago." I ask Coyote, "Who did Planet Earth request the help from?"

Coyote says, "From all of the Divine Souls on Planet Earth, as we are the co-creators of this planet, the Divine energy is inside all of our souls." Coyote tells us that long ago, Planet Earth asked every single living thing, on a soul level, if She could intervene to save Herself. Ninety-three percent responded favourably". Planet Earth has been waiting, patiently, as She knows how to wait. However, the time is upon us, as the human race is totally dysfunctional, very unbalanced and compartmentalized. "How are most people unbalanced?" I ask. Coyote reveals that the human body is bombarded with different frequencies which travel through the body and weaken the nervous system, destroying DNA and the human body. This occurs day and night, as we turn our world into a 24/7 retail experience.

First the radio, then radar, then x-rays, microwaves, cell phones, cell towers, big brother camera systems, hand held technology, and *(available soon)* eye implants for online games, bionic body parts, and computers that can think for you. We are being turned into walking robots, with more and more metal attached to the body. What about the microchip technology planned soon, to turn us into our own personal walking computers? What are they going to do next, plug us into a mainframe computer? Maybe they already have, through the mass media via TV and computers.

Coyote continues, "The microchips have been harming our fellow animals. Do your research. Your cats and dogs are now sick. The microchips cause tumours and are slowly killing us. Stop micro-chipping us and stop using radio collars on my relations. Do you want to turn the animals into robots as well? We do not need your so-called help. You the humans need our help. We are still connected to Planet Earth. She tells us when to go to a safe place. In all major earthquakes, hurricanes, heavy flooding and tsunamis, the animals leave the area, as they pick up the changes *(message)* in the atmosphere, which is from our mother, Planet Earth. Your species, the humans, needs this knowledge."

"Weather, like you have never seen before, will come and cleanse this planet in many places, as it has been doing over the last few years. Man has created imbalance in the first place, and Nature needs to heal this world. Does your soul still commune with the Planet? Will She send you a message and keep you safe?" There is an old Native American saying; ***The further man is from nature, the further man is from his Soul.***

Coyote explains that human beings' ways bring great sadness to the world, energetically. We humans, sit in front of televisions and computers all day. We create our view of the world through mass media news channels, which are owned by the fake elite, who feed us doom and gloom. The truth is, we are deceived and uneducated about how our minds create our own experiences. If doom and gloom goes into our minds via the news, then we absorb those images and project them out again, unwittingly creating that doom and gloom in our own lives.

Therefore, turning off the TV is a great start. At least stop watching mainstream news. The news is a version of reality that is purposely created to upset, annoy and irritate you. We, then, are sending out *(manifesting)* more of the same. Why do the fake elite want us annoyed and irritated, you may ask? When you are annoyed, do you make good judgments, feel powerful and in control? No, you make mistakes, become aggressive and stressed. You are made to feel powerless and that keeps you projecting out the same. It makes you powerless, and them powerful.

The people of this magnificent planet need to come together to save this world, and first, we need to stop killing each other. This society is based on war and terror. War is really a cover for competition for resources. First, land and water, then oil and gas, and next it will be people. Terra is the Latin name for Earth, funny how terror and terra sounds exactly the same. Are we are being indoctrinated with a play on words?

"War on terror = War on terra."[4]

We hear this 'War on Terror' statement constantly. Do we

4 A quote from Jordan Maxwell

object to using these words that continue to create constant war? I do not think we are aware of what is drummed into our heads.

Over the next five years, *up to 2013*, this world will experience many great changes to our planet. Magical happenings bring wonderment and awe back into our souls. A huge soul retrieval *(healing)* will be happening. Soul retrieval is when some of your energy is returned to you. So the human race will receive healing and a chance to get back their lost personal power. This means humans will suddenly start to feel whole and balanced again. Solar flares will knock out the energy grids. A solar flare is an explosion of charged particles that can devastate satellites, power grids and the magnetic field around the Earth. Huge fireworks in the sky is how you humans will see this event. For many years it has been known that our Sun gives off these powerful explosions, also known as sun spots, which go in cycles. They contain millions of times more energy than an atomic bomb.

During 'Cycle 23' the world saw the largest solar flares ever recorded from our Sun. 'Cycle 23' ended in March, 2007. The Sun entered 'Cycle 24' in August 2007, which NASA has predicted will be 50% stronger than 'Cycle 23'. 'Cycle 24' is due to peak between the years of 2011 and 2012.[5]

Over the next 4 years, we can expect some whopper flares and therefore, larger Earth-changing events, such as more earthquakes, volcanoes and hurricanes. This also means

5 http://www.newscientist.com/article/dn13769-does-the-earths-magnetic-field-cause-suicides.html
http://www.nasa.gov/centers/goddard/news/topstory/2008/pipsqueak_star.html

we humans will be bombarded with even more charged particles than ever, via the same geomagnetic storms from the Sun, and more changes within ourselves. The charged particles from the Sun affect the Earth's weather by affecting the Earth's magnetic field. Animals and humans have a magnetic field which surrounds them in a similar way as the magnetic field surrounds the Earth.

Our ancestors *(Druids, Mayan & indigenous peoples)* knew there was a connection between the Sun and other celestial events which affected humans and animals on Planet Earth.

Electricity and energy problems will actually be a blessing, and even though we will have to adjust to the changes, the human body will benefit. We will be returning to living in nature. It is important to stop all this bombardment of different frequencies to let us once again live naturally, in nature, and with nature.

I thanked Coyote and asked her to stay. She smiled at me and nodded her head and goes to sit beside Chief Black Elk, who wants to play with her and cuddle her. I send violet and pale blue mist to cover the Mare, and this helps release the group of humans, the fake elite have now completely vanished. Suddenly, huge rain clouds form, it starts to rain heavily, it becomes very dark, and massive bolts of silver lightening crackle very loudly across the dark blue sky. We all look up in awe. Many bright blue and purple lightening bolts light up the entire sky and join the dance with the rainstorm. Sitting Bull laughs at the huge electrical storms that start to encircle the Medicine Wheel. The rainstorm is very loud and very powerful.

The Mare is prancing around and bucking. Unafraid, she dances in the rainstorm. She represents Planet Earth's heart. She knows how to love everyone. She sends *True Love* for everyone, while she dances in the rain storm. She is very happy and bows down her head, tossing her copper mane, to honour all of us on Planet Earth at this time. She tells us to welcome the Earth cleansing. The Mare goes and stands by the North to be with Chief Sitting Bull. She wants us to listen to her friend Grizzly Bear.

Grizzly Bear Speaks About Original Spirituality

I called to Grizzly Bear, the Spirit Keeper of the West and the element of Earth, to show us how our planet is feeling spiritually at this time. Sun Bear and I stand in the West singing a song of healing for Grizzly Bear, as she is very weak and we cannot see her. It starts to rain heavily again. I see mud everywhere, I see a large spinning vortex opening up and wanting to swallow all the buildings, roads, dams and highways, knowing that these things keep us from nature and connecting with Planet Earth.

I call again to Grizzly Bear, I see a shimmer of what used to be a big strong beautiful brown Grizzly Bear, with grey flecks that once sparkled like silver, and she is fading in and out like a ghost. I ask Grizzly Bear if she wants to receive healing in my Medicine Wheel. Grizzly Bear, shaking her head, looks down and states, "It's all backwards", and she is very upset. Sun Bear goes to pick her up and carries her into the Medicine Wheel. She is very small, with very little fur, Sun Bear is concerned and I let him do healing on her.

When she is looking better, we ask her to talk to us about the human soul. We are told the following:

"Human beings have given away their power through religion, a subtle, spiritually devastating form of mind control. Religion implies servitude to another human being, whether it is a priest, vicar, rabbi or guru."

"Do you really want to entrust your soul to a man *(usually)* you barely know, who wears strange outfits and works for the church? Really, you give away your own sovereign right to be a powerful magical co-creator with Planet Earth, because some guy in a purple/black dress *(to represent the feminine)* says so."

"Attending a church and begging to God to answer all your prayers? Yes, let's constantly create loads of desperation, by begging on our knees every Sunday, creating energetically desperate human beings. Great!"

"There is a higher Divine Power. It wants you to take full responsibility for your lives, not wait around hoping for changes. Be the changes you want to see. Make things happen."

"Research the history of the religious orders. If you go back far enough, it has always been about controlling the population and the money. The focus was shifted to there being only *'one'* life. Reincarnation was abolished to scare you into complete submission. Do as we say in this life or you will go to hell for eternity. Very clever. The churches are extremely powerful and wealthy institutions. Why is this? Do they have to pay a premium to get your soul into heaven? Is there a secret toll, that from the goodness of their hearts, they spare us the worry and the cost? I think not."

Grizzly Bear continues, "The original spiritually of the Human Being, your Original Divine Souls, has been tampered with, or rather inverted. You have all suffered extreme soul loss, due mainly to the fake elite's fake religious conditioning. To divert our attention away from Nature and towards being controlled, unnatural, robots, constantly fighting over religion, land and resources."

This is what religion was set up to accomplish. To separate us, to divide us. To ultimately weaken all of humanity over a very long period of time. To destroy humanity and this planet, through biological and chemical wars, destroying the environment.

You need to listen to your soul's inner intelligence. We need to stop feeling separate from each other, to realise we are all from the same planet, we are all human beings. We need to work on ourselves and heal the entire journey of our soul. You can save your own soul. Which helps everyone on this planet at this time, as the more we love ourselves the more love we create and add to this world. We are all one, as you heal yourself, you heal all of this world. We are love. We are God.

Grizzly Bear is eating healing berries and fruit. She is becoming more solid, I give her some hands-on healing, using violet and pale pink. She starts to giggle. She does a silly dance and gives me a big hug. She wants to tell humans to go and heal your soul and get back your power. Your power is True Love for yourself. Grizzly Bear is now sitting on the blanket snuggling up to Sun Bear.

White Buffalo Warns That Nothing Is Natural Anymore

Sitting Bull and I call to White Buffalo, the Spirit Keeper of the North, the element of Air, which represents the physical world and the future. The Great North Wind suddenly appears, the trees are swaying quite violently. I hear in the distance a stampede of White Buffaloes. The loudness grows and a rumbling of the ground can be heard as it starts to shake. In the distance, I see many volcanoes erupting, sending ash and moulten lava into the air.

I spot the leader of the White Buffaloes, trotting towards me. She is dressed in a very strange fancy dress outfit, with a party paper hat on, carrying loads of designer shopping bags. I wondered who she was dressed up as. She arrives and informs me that she is dressed as *Little Bo Peep* who has lost her sheep! And doesn't know where to find them! I think that means most people are acting like lost sheep!

On her back piled high are white goods. Unbelievably, she is carrying a fridge, a freezer, a cooker, a video, a DVD player, a TV, a microwave, a computer, an iPod and a cell phone. She has medical equipment as well, as if an IV has been put into her front right leg. She is very overweight and has wobbly legs that are very weak. In addition, I think she is drunk, as her eyes are crossed. She has lots of pressure in her head. Hmm, she is not well or coherent at all. Remind you of anyone?

I ask White Buffalo to enter the Medicine Wheel. A large silver lightening bolt strikes to clear her from all the man-made items.

All that I see now, is a beautiful strong pure White Buffalo, standing among the pile of man-made items, which immediately shrink and she kicks them happily into the sacred fire.

White Buffalo starts speaking. She asks that we listen to her, and to the animals and elements that wish to speak to us *(humans)* about the current state of this beautiful world.

She wants to see us reject the current model of industrialization, and to create a holistic approach to resources and lifestyles. Unfortunately, the third world countries now see it as their time to industrialize, yet, going back to the land and cleaning up the water supplies is the only way forward. She urges us to go back to the land.

White Buffalo says, "This world is a shop, when it should be a land of paradise. You need to stop buying stuff from the shop. As consumers, human beings have ultimate power. You seem to be unaware of this. You humans buy the products. Stop buying the products. This is your real power at this time, even your food that is not organic is cloned versions of the original. Nothing is natural anymore. Go back to nature."

"Don't buy genetically modified foods. It is designed to genetically modify humans. Do it now. Vote with your wallet and see the industry change, overnight. In addition, read what additives are in those prepackaged meals. Why are you humans eating so many chemicals?"

"Home cooking, starting from scratch, is the only way

you can truly see what's in your meals, so learn to cook from scratch and buy locally grown food. This is very important. Financially, you are helping your local area. All food holds the vibration of the place in which it was grown. It is best consumed there, yet we shop and buy products from all over the world, which when consumed, confuses the frequency of our bodies and weakens the human body."

"You need to demand healthier solutions to packaging as well. You need to reduce plastic wrapping. Most products are individually wrapped, and then re-wrapped and then boxed! Why? Reduce excess packaging now. Stop buying individually wrapped items. Make a difference and start today. No more manufacturing of plastic bags, plastic bottles and metal cans. How can you do this? What did you humans use before plastic! Use glass and recycle. This needs to become the norm."

"Go to a local area that needs cleaning up and get on with cleaning the rubbish up. Once it is clean, take a photograph of the area. Look at this photo every day to anchor in the rubbish free area, you will notice people stop dropping litter there. That would be a good place to start. Involve children in looking after green areas. Cleaning up litter is the first step to healing this planet."

We thanked White Buffalo. She now asks that we talk to her friend, the Turtle.

Can You Help the Oceans?

Turtle walks into my Medicine Wheel and shows me a vision. In my imagination, I see her swimming frantically, as if she wants to get away from a deadly enemy. I see many men and large fishing boats after her. She is breathing rapidly, and is very nervous of being killed. This is how Planet Earth feels at this time.

I get Turtle to sit with me and receive hands-on light blue healing mist, filling her and Planet Earth with peace.

"All the fish in the sea are having trouble breathing. The oxygen levels are dropping, and that is why the solar flares will help create big natural storms to put back the oxygen. If we cannot breathe, we will not procreate, and then the fish stocks will diminish altogether all over the world. This will lead to mass starvation for humans."

"You must clean up the pollution in the oceans. Stop carelessly dumping small plastic lighters, combs, bags and food wrappings in our waters. If you refuse to buy these plastic items, they will not end up in the ocean. It actually is that simple. Can you help the oceans? Can you refuse to buy these particular plastic items?"

"We are also tired of the continuous pulsing noises that make the ocean beds gently shake. The sonar waves are making us experience constant tinnitus. We end up in the wrong place and loose many of our family when we travel across great distances. The beautiful Dolphins *(purity)* and Whales *(experience)* are sad and show us how sad they are by turning up on shores beached. We make statements with our bodies when we are tired of the constant noise pollution. It is a relief to die. This is very serious. Your Navy and Military can be persuaded, put pressure on them for us. Then small pockets of silence can be set up for us to find relief."

Native tribes used to be the only ones that sent the Planet Earth healing energy. Now many people from all walks of life realize they can send Her healing and love, and She feels this healing, this love. I call to the Great Spirit, Great Mystery to send down violet healing mist and send it all over the entire oceans of this beautiful world. We send a magical net to scoop up all the plastic and remove it, energetically, from the oceans. We see many scuba divers collecting the plastic items and burning them in the sacred fire. We see all the fish in the sea smiling and breathing in pure oxygen. We send love to all the beings of the sea.

We The Trees Are Here To Protect You

At each of the four directions are small Japanese bonsai trees, Oak, Cedar, Pine and Maple. The four trees start to grow and become so big that I decide to fly up to the top of the oak tree. Oak speaks for the world's trees: "We see many of our forests completely devastated by massive forest fires and monumental logging. We have very bad news, if you continue to cut us down, only 30 percent of the trees will be living in 20 years time. Know this, we are here purely for the animals and the structure of the land. You humans have broken the soul connection. We are nearly dead to you. All the trees in the world are saddened by the cutting of life force energy that we were holding for all of you. This energy is moving to other worlds. Only some humans will be able to stay and play here."

"The indigenous tribes of the world are having their habitat taken away. We, the trees, are here to protect you, providing materials to build structures to shield you from the weather. We are here to clean the air, to feed you with our nuts and fruits, and heal you with our medicines. Yet, we have been seen as something to cut down and destroy."

"Why are you cutting down your future breath? If you live for today it means you die tomorrow."

"The forest fires are out of control and you will see many more fires all over this planet in the next few years. We are dying fast and you don't care! Why don't you manage the forests as your ancestors did? Why have you forgotten to love and honour the trees, especially in North America, Canada, Europe and Asia? Millions, yes millions of trees no longer exist! What have you done? In the long term, our forests must remain. It is paramount to the survival of the human race. Please help us. We urge you to plant more trees *(more friends)* for your future."

"Every single person on the planet needs to plant a tree, a herb and a flower for every year of their life, and do it now. You will be making your tomorrows, and making more friends for the humans. There is little time. Act now!"

Plant trees, herbs and flowers, which are local species to your area. As more are planted, it will send love to all the trees, herbs and flowers. When you love and respect a tree, all trees feel your love. Love the trees, herbs and flowers and they will stay. I send love, rainbow healing mist and future energy to every tree, herb and flower in the world. We thanked Oak, who shrank back to a small Bonsai Tree.

The Rain Is Crying

I flew up into the Air and called to the Rain and the Wind to tell us their story. Rain was crying, believe it or not. Rain speaks, "I'm dirty and heavy, stop spraying chemicals which are hurting me. A massive global chemical spraying operation, using a large fleet of many hundreds of aircraft, seems to operate over most countries of the world. It is now severely damaging ALL life on Earth. These chemicals are very dangerous to all life on Earth. If I am filled with chemicals, I spread death all over the planet. I am life, let me be life. Why are you destroying me? I want to get away. Why do you poison this planet?"

"All these nuclear bomb tests! I understand that over 50 have been detonated in our atmosphere. What have been the benefits to mankind, to this planet? Was it worth it? Has mankind advanced by these hideous poisonous ways or weapons of mass destruction?"

Did you know that once after a nuclear experiment, which created new electromagnetic belts in the atmosphere, the caribou mysteriously failed to migrate for the first time in 3000 years? A warning perhaps of how the migration of animals, fish and birds may be affected by disturbances to electromagnetic fields - and of the potential impact this could have on every living thing."

"Also, every single rocket launched puts billions of gallons of fuel particles into the air. Everyone is too busy watching the rocket to look at the profound amount of poisons that cannot be cleaned up, ever! What are you humans doing to this beautiful place?"

"With the additional problem, in the last 50 years or so, the fake elite, your governments, have played around with the weather. Did you know? Every year, China launches thousands of rockets and artillery shells into the sky. Through its Weather Modification Programme, China hopes to control the forces behind rain. What do you think your own country is doing to this beautiful world?"

I send deep cleansing to all the rain, using a violet and pale blue cleansing potion that clears the toxins and chemicals out of the rain. I separate the metals and dissolve them in love and justice. The rain starts to become big and clear, like a massive rainbow coloured raindrop, she smiles. She says thanks for the release from all of the horrible pollutants.

The Wind Is Haunted

I call to the Wind, and she is sniffing too. She's thick in some places and weak and thin in others, and she is tightly held by a strange metallic energy in the sky. Wind tells me, "I am getting ready to dance with the rain."

"I am haunted by a dull humming that slices into my being. HAARP is responsible, research this." HAARP *(America's High-frequency Active Auroral Research Programme)* a multimillion dollar *'civilian'* installation, hidden away in Alaska, ostensibly intended to *'alter the performance of communications and surveillance systems'*. Seemingly innocent enough, until she explains that this grid of 180 transmission towers is funded by the military and is part of the 'Star

Wars' defence network. HAARP, and its linked brother projects are, she says, known to the military as *'ionosphere modification facilities'.*"[6]

Wind tells us that there are ethical questions and Human Rights Concerns regarding HAARP. There are a diversity of popular theories surrounding HAARP, crediting it with being a secret missile tracking/defence system, earthquake tracking *(or causing)* system, weather control, mind control, or having some other secret function. We see the three main facilities, HAARP, HIPAS near Fairbanks, Alaska, and the ARECIBO Observatory in Puerto Rico, with big signs saying CLOSED AND ABANDONED FOREVER!

I call the healing energy of the rainbows to help the rain and wind. We see the wind start to heal, and once again, she is thick, strong, and able to move freely through the air. We send violet, gold and silver healing mist to the rain, the wind, the sky and the entire atmosphere of this beautiful planet.

We Call To The Mountains Of This World

The Mountains of Planet Earth wish to speak about the mining and the feelings of abuse and pain. It is like someone taking your appendix. Hey, if its part of you, you may

---

6 An ionospheric modification facility is a heater, an array of 180 massive antennas which are used for heating the ionosphere (SKY), and which can create artificial aurora borealis (a natural light display). The United States has three ionospheric heating facilities: the HAARP, the HIPAS near FAIRBANKS, Alaska and (currently offline for modifications) one at the Arecibo Observatory in Puerto Rico. The ionospheric is the uppermost part of the atmosphere, distinguished because it is ionized by solar radiation. It plays an important part in atmospheric electricity and forms the inner edge of the magnetosphere.

wish to keep it on some level.

"I *(the Mountains)* am being tirelessly ripped open by big explosions and illegal mining. My skin is ripped off and the pillaging begins. All the metals and precious stones you have taken out of me. What have you used me for? How has it made your life better? I cannot see how by wearing my gold, silver or copper to make you look more appealing, has made any real difference."

"Why have you stolen my body that makes me look beautiful? Who said you could have it? Did you ask? My body has been punched and prodded, it has been scooped out, and the funny thing is, most of what you take from me is discarded. Waste and water consumption are being excessively used, your mines are poisoning the world water supplies as well. Why do this? The Indigenous people, who know how to love Planet Earth, are being thrown off their land and are resorting to eating poisoned fish. The mercury and pollution are making the local rivers, as well as the mines, one of the biggest ecological problems now."

"The diamonds, precious gem stones and crystals that you take out of me, keep harmony with the structure and frequency of my being. They are parts of my soul. It is like someone taking your selenium out of your brain. The clarity fades as you take more of my soul, distributing them all over the planet on people's fingers. It is scattering my soul, my sacred power. It is in the wrong place now. It is yet another way to destroy Planet Earth. It is time to find beauty within, not with gold or diamonds. You are not helping my pulse of life if you carry it to different parts of the world.

Please stop it."

"Planet Earth wishes to acknowledge that some humans do understand the true healing properties of certain metals, diamonds, gems and crystals. They are respectful and seek permission before use and activate them correctly to do their work, which isn't sitting on someone's finger, only to be admired."

I send pale pink healing and love to the Mountains and the mines. They are sad. I call to the Volcanoes, "Tell me your wisdom"

The Volcanoes Come To Tell Us Their Wisdom

"Before pollution, say 250 years ago, we *(the Volcanoes)* were here to keep the soil rich in vibrant nutrients to help all plant life, which feeds and supports all life."

"Volcanoes help release certain stress points in Planet Earths' body. Also, they were places that could release gases and heat if needed. Now pollution has actually cooled the planet. Global warming is a scam. We the Volcanoes are being manipulated by HAARP and are getting ready to blast!"

"The powers that hold the reins of the world until 2013 want humans to feel bad *(meaning pay for)* all the pollution, yet you were deceived. No one was honest with you. Greed and money were the name of the game. My fossil fuels never ever needed to be taken. Now I have big holes inside me that are causing me to sway and lose balance."

"Many years ago, and again recently, several alternative free energy inventions appeared and vanished, kept hidden from the public. Why? Because the fossil fuel companies were just making too much money to care about long term effects. None of the coal or oil needed to be taken. It takes millions of years to make fossil fuels, yet you humans had been obsessed with consuming at least 50% of the planet's entire supply in a matter of 100 years. Why are you doing this? Eighty-five percent of all the energy that 'runs' this planet is via fossil fuels, not a good idea for the future of this planet. You need to learn to do without fossil fuels, really, to help clean up the mess."

"Cars have single-handedly caused much of the health and weight problems in modern people. Sitting in a metal box cuts you off from nature. Yes, you look out the window at a beautiful scene in 2D, but unless you are sitting outside in fresh air 3D, you remain disconnected from nature, which leads to disconnection from your soul, disconnected from your true power."

I send pale green and ice blue healing mist to all the mountains and volcanoes, filling the holes and spaces inside of Planet Earth with whatever is needed to bring back balance to the entire inner structure of our planet. I thanked all the Power Animals and Planet Earth for speaking to us. We thanked Great Spirit, Great Mystery.

I have seen the future, Planet Earth is travelling into the *Age of Aquarius*, with magic and True Love. Planet Earth urges us to go and find our power within. To go and find True Love, by listening to our soul's inner intelligence, to become magical universal human beings. For your Great Adventure is about to begin...

Addendum

Good Words To Live By

Native American Traditional Code of Ethics

Originally published the *'Inter-Tribal Times'*
October of 1994.

Each morning upon rising, and each evening before sleeping, give thanks for the life within you and for all life, for the good things the Creator has given you and for the opportunity to grow a little more each day. Consider your thoughts and actions of the past day and seek for the courage and strength to be a better person. Seek for the things that will benefit others (everyone).

Respect: Respect means 'To feel or show honour or esteem for someone or something; to consider the well being of, or to treat someone or something with deference or courtesy'. Showing respect is a basic law of life.

Treat every person, the tiniest child to the oldest elder, with respect at all times.

Special respect should be given to Elders, Parents, Teachers, and

Community Leaders.

No person should be made to feel 'put down' by you; avoid hurting other hearts, as you would avoid a deadly poison.

Touch nothing that belongs to someone else (especially Sacred Objects) without permission, or an understanding between you.

Respect the privacy of every person; never intrude on a person's quiet moment or personal space.

Never walk between people that are conversing.

Never interrupt people who are conversing.

Speak in a soft voice, especially when you are in the presence of Elders, strangers or others to whom special respect is due.

Do not speak unless invited to do so at gatherings where Elders are present (except to ask what is expected of you, should you be in doubt).

Never speak about others in a negative way, whether they are present or not.

Treat the Earth and all of her aspects as your mother. Show deep respect for the mineral world, the plant world, and the animal world. Do nothing to pollute our Mother, rise up with wisdom to defend her.

Show deep respect for the beliefs and religion of others.

Listen with courtesy to what others say, even if you feel that what they are saying is worthless. Listen with your heart.

Respect the wisdom of the people in council. Once you give an idea to a council meeting it no longer belongs to you. It belongs to the people. Respect demands that you listen intently to the ideas of others in council and that you do not insist that your idea prevail. Indeed you should freely support the ideas of others if they are true and good, even if those ideas are quite different from the ones you have contributed. The clash of ideas brings forth the Spark of Truth.

Once a council has decided something in unity, respect demands that no one speak secretly against what has been decided. If the council has made an error, that error will become apparent to everyone in its own time.

Be truthful at all times, and under all conditions.

Always treat your guests with honour and consideration. Give of your best food, your best blankets, the best part of your house, and your best service to your guests.

The hurt of one is the hurt of all; the honour of one is the honour of all.

Receive strangers and outsiders with a loving heart and as members of the human family.

All the races and tribes in the world are like the different coloured flowers of one meadow. All are beautiful. As children of the Creator they must all be respected.

To serve others, to be of some use to family, community, nation, and the world are one of the main purposes for which human beings have been created. Do not fill yourself with your own affairs and forget your most important talks. True happiness comes only to those who dedicate their lives to the service of others.

Observe moderation and balance in all things.

Know those things that lead to your well being, and those things that lead to your destruction.

Listen to and follow the guidance given to your heart. Expect guidance to come in many forms; in prayer, in dreams, in times of quiet solitude, and in the words and deeds of wise Elders and friends.

Lakota Sioux Prayer Song

If you say or sing this out loud, you will be blessed by Wankan-Tanka, a Native American name for Planet Earth. Sing it to all your Power Animals, it is the start of your Great Adventure.

Be silly and have fun. That's the biggest secret in the world, WE ARE LOVE. You can remember, if you want to. Do you want to remember? It's fun. Go on!

Friend do this! Friend do this! Friend do this!
If you do this your Grandfather will see you
When you stand within the holy circle
Think of me when you place the sacred tobacco in the pipe
If you do this He will give you all that you ask for

Friend do this! Friend do this! Friend do this!
If you do this your Grandfather will see you
When you stand within the holy circle
Send your voice to Wankan-Tanka
If you do this He will give you all that you desire

Friend do this! Friend do this! Friend do this!
If you do this your Grandfather will see you
When you stand within the holy circle
Crying and with tears send your voice to Wankan-Tanka
If you do this you will have all that you desire

Friend do this! Friend do this! Friend do this!
If you do this your Grandfather will see you
When you stand within the sacred hoop
Raise your hand to Wankan-Tanka
Do this and He will bestow upon you all that you desire.

Given to the Sioux, by White Calf Buffalo Woman, a Spiritual deity, to help join all nations of this world in peace.

"Ho! And so it is."

Tribal Love, How to Love Everyone

This is how you do it. How to create Peaceful Tribes on Earth. Planet Earth and I talk a lot. This is what she tells me: "There are, pretty much, two groups in this world. The first is the unawakened, the iPod loony, who dont care that the forests, our future breath, is being destroyed. They just want the latest gadget. The other group is the awakened. However, they seem to be angry at each other, or the governments, the multinational companies, the world banks, the 'New World Order' as well as the unawakened. Neither group serves me. I want you to realise that every thought, feeling and action creates your tomorrows. Start with love and end with love. Follow 'Good words to live by' and have some respect for all that graces this world. Are you perfect? Love all of yourself, which means everybody who is here, as anything you see in this world that you don't like is a reflection of you, or you would not attract it into your life. We all make mistakes and all mistakes can be forgiven. Be a loving Powerful Creator at this very special and magical time. That will give me the creative energy and love I seek."

So this is Planet Earth's humble opinion for us humans to ponder over! Love everyone, even your worst enemy! Our planet is a place for people to share, to find and explore a peaceful way to love everyone. Anger serves no man, woman, child, planet, or blade of grass. Even, righteous anger. Anger is anger. Don't you agree, Yes!

Learn how to use the Native American Medicine Wheel to create a peaceful life for yourself and others, and many more peaceful solutions. I hope everyone will help beautiful Planet Earth. Let us see if we can have some fun, too!

Continue Your Shamanic Journey

Now you've read this book, go and visit our websites *www.samanthawilliams.co.uk* and *www.marcwilliams.co.uk* to continue your journey. You will find regular updates and wonderful information and inspiration. Get a free Power Animal reading, and listen to the music available from Marc on his site, it is true medicine for your heart, mind, body and soul.

2825814R00094

Printed in Great Britain
by Amazon.co.uk, Ltd.,
Marston Gate.